JOEY

JOSEPH JOHN DEACON

JOEY

CHARLES SCRIBNER'S SONS
NEW YORK

Library of Congress Cataloging in Publication Data
Deacon, Joseph John.
  Joey.
  Published in 1974 under title: Tongue tied.
  Autobiographical.
  1. Physically handicapped—Personal narratives.
2. Cerebral palsy—Personal narratives.   I. Title.
RD796.D4A35   1976   362.2'1'0924 [B]   75-15452
ISBN 0-684-14474-3

1 3 5 7 9 11 13 15 17 19 V/C 20 18 16 14 12 10 8 6 4 2

Printed in the United States of America

Photographs by Robert Brook

INTRODUCTION

ALTHOUGH THE STORY IN THIS BOOK IS WITHOUT DOUBT THE creative work of one man, it was a team of four, inseparable and devoted friends for many years and all residents of St. Lawrence's Hospital, that brought it to birth.

The author is Joey Deacon, born in 1920, a spastic with all four limbs affected. He spent the first eight years of his life at home except that during this time he was in and out of hospitals for operations on his spastic limbs. In 1928, after six months in Queen Mary's Hospital, Carshalton, he was admitted to St. Lawrence's and spent the first years of his life there in the children's wards. Joey is the most physically handicapped of the four and still lives permanently by day in a wheelchair, dependent on his three friends for his journey to work each day and his excursions around and about the hospital. The remarkable feature about Joey, as we consider his book, is his very deficient speech resulting from his spasticity. In fact, a stranger meeting him for the first time would be slow to believe that he ever said an intelligible word. In response to a question he will grimace and salivate and make incomprehensible sounds; even the staff who have known him for years still find themselves unable to understand more than a little.

But not so Ernie Roberts. Ernie was born in 1928, also a spastic and also the subject of many early operations on his limbs. He was admitted to St. Lawrence's in 1938 and being only ten years old at the time was, like Joey, a resident at first of the children's wards.

Transfer to the adult wards took place at St. Lawrence's when children reached the age of sixteen. Thus Joey was transferred in 1936 but Ernie did not follow him until eight years later, in 1944. Exact dates of some of the events are now difficult to determine with absolute certainty (and there are some errors in the dates as recalled by the author), but 1944 does seem to have been an important year for three members of the foursome. It was in this year that Tom Blackburn, the least handicapped of the four, was admitted at the age of eighteen. Born in 1926 at Greenwich with no physical handicaps, he spent some years at home until the death of his father, and then, because of his mother's ill health, was adopted by an aunt. For three years before admission he worked in a sawmill, but after his mother's death, hospital admission became inevitable.

The meetings between these three men, Joey, Ernie, and Tom, which led to their lasting friendship, occurred while they lived together on Male Ward C1 and worked together in the "wool-sorting shop" (no longer in existence).

Ernie was completely unable to walk and coped with his spasticity by crawling about on hands and feet. It was Tom who took him in hand and taught him to walk. Today Ernie still uses a chair for longer distances, with Tom pushing; but shorter distances he can manage on his feet—and he never crawls.

In a remarkably short time ("a week" says Ernie), Ernie

[6]

could understand what Joey was trying to say. This was made clear to the staff one day when Ernie informed them that Joey had expressed a wish to go home for a Christmas holiday. From that day Ernie and Joey became inseparable friends.

Michael Sangster was added to the team in 1946, when he was admitted to St. Lawrence's at the age of sixteen. He entered the same ward as the others and because he had no physical handicap he was soon asked by Ernie to help with Joey and his wheelchair.

So the quartet was complete, all four with varying degrees of mental handicap and two severely physically handicapped as well, but, as a team, living a full social life at St. Lawrence's and working together in the sheltered workshop. Tom and Michael could well survive in an outside community hostel but this is the last thing they would consider because it would mean breaking up the group.

In 1958 Joey Deacon was admitted to the "sick ward" with tuberculosis of the lung, from which happily he made a full recovery. One day while he lay ill a member of the staff, Mr. Leslie Atkins, at that time a staff nurse and now senior nursing officer in charge of training, told Joey of how another spastic had written a book using his toes to hold his pen. Would not Joey also like to think about the possibility of doing a similar thing? Joey thought about it to himself and continued to think about it for the next twelve years though no one realized what was going on in his mind.

Then one Saturday in 1970 the silently fermenting idea seemed to have reached maturity. Joey said to Ernie, "I'm going to write my story," and Ernie proceeded just as unspectacularly to arrange that it could be done. He obtained pen and paper, but he cannot read or write. However, Michael can, not easily or accurately but well enough, and he became the scribe for the operation.

So it began with Joey slowly, incoherently, as it would seem to an outside observer, starting to tell his tale. Ernie alone could understand, and he would sit watching Joey's face intently and listening and then turning away and repeating what he had heard to Michael who laboriously wrote it down.

It is at this point that mention must be made of the staff and the part they have played. So many have been involved in a small way and for varying periods that it is impossible to recall them all by name. Two however had a major role, one which lasted throughout the writing of the book; both are still closely associated with the four principal men of this story. They are the charge nurses responsible for Male Ward C1, Mr. Ronald Atkins and Mr. John Eaton. Under their leadership a good community has been developed within a very old ward still urgently needing rejuvenation and holding a population of over forty severely physically and mentally handicapped men, many in wheelchairs for much of their lives. They have found time over the years to give special support and encouragement to the four men of this story.

So it was, of course, to them that Michael turned with his rough script as it was completed day by day, and it was they who looked the script over and rewrote it, supplying the punctuation and underlining capital letters, and

[8]

who corrected errors of spelling, while at the same time being careful to make no essential alteration in the substance of the contents. Later, Mr. Christopher Ring, a voluntary worker, also helped in these corrections.

Before long it was decided that the written pages should be typed and that the responsibility for this side of the operation should be given to Tom. Ernie bought a plastic typewriter which soon proved to be too fragile and so Tom bought a secondhand one that was suitable for the purpose. But Tom had never typed a word in his life. Besides, he could neither read nor write. With the same quiet determination that has characterized each stage of this work, Tom taught himself to type laboriously, letter by letter, using one finger of each hand. Then, in order to communicate to Tom, Joey took the script and read out each portion (also letter by letter) carefully noting where the punctuation marks and capital letters occurred, and Ernie repeated the letters to Tom.

To reduce the number of errors in this elaborate process, Tom devised a special code for the alphabet; this code is given here in full on the following page. The first six letters are represented by the names of male wards in St. Lawrence's. The personal names are those of people Tom has known, including some of his past and present girlfriends at St. Lawrence's. The phonetic character of his alphabet is shown by letters Q and Y.

After Ernie had named aloud a letter for Tom to type, Tom would repeat it also aloud using the code. Ernie would say "F" and Tom would repeat "F for F-one" and type it; Ernie would say "O" and Tom would repeat

"O for Orange" and type it; Ernie would say "R" and Tom "R for Robert" and type it; and so the word "for" would be completed. This would continue for an hour or two on many evenings of each week, a page or two a day, with breaks only for holidays, sickness, or after a hard day's work elsewhere. The day's typing would again be taken to the charge nurses of the ward for rechecking.

There were plenty of problems of course. On one occasion the pages were found to have been wrongly numbered and it took a whole day to get things sorted out again. The typewriter broke down several times and there were delays while it was repaired or another one borrowed.

But finally in May 1971, after fourteen months, the task was at an end; and since that time only a few pages have been added.

Tom's Alphabet

A	for A-one	H	for Harry	O	for Orange	V	for Victor
B	for B-one	I	for Ivy	P	for Peter	W	for Window
C	for C-one	J	for Jack	Q	for Cucumber	X	for "Oxo"
D	for D-one	K	for Kettle	R	for Robert	Y	for Willie
E	for E-one	L	for Linda	S	for Sharon	Z	for Zebra
F	for F-one	M	for Mother	T	for Terry		
G	for Gloria	N	for Neddie	U	for U-boat		

Now that the task is over and the book published it becomes an important question to ask, "To what end?" No one is going to hail the work as a literary masterpiece, although its very simplicity does have a real charm. But the book has many values.

If nothing else it shows what can be done by a severely

physically and mentally handicapped resident of an institution. It should also help us to appreciate that those who live in such institutions have a point of view of their own, have feelings and aspirations which they not only have the right to express but have very often the capability of so doing if they have a fair chance. The day must surely come when we do listen to what is said by those who depend upon us to a greater or lesser extent for care, when we take them into our planning and even our conferences—since it is for them and their needs that we say we plan and on their behalf that we confer. Anything that will encourage us to listen with proper humility is worthwhile.

We are in danger of allowing to lie dormant so much of the potential of our mentally and physically handicapped residents, not because we want to, but because out of our traditionally custodial role has arisen a tendency to pessimism about our handicapped fellows. Human beings, including the mentally handicapped, may well become only what is expected of them by those around. Maybe this book will help all those whose professional interests bring them in touch with the mentally handicapped to expect more.

Above all, of course, this book is an example of what can be achieved by cooperative effort. Here four men came, almost without outside influence, to support each other in the most dramatic way, each supplying what the others lacked. The result was for all a surprisingly full and contented life, as well as the production of creative work impossible for any one of them alone. Moreover, this book required the cooperation of residents and staff together—

including nurses, social workers and voluntary workers. Perhaps there is a nucleus here for our thinking about new ways in which the mentally handicapped may survive in society, for it may be possible to form groups of handicapped people who compensate for one another's deficiencies and as a result can function effectively with minimal professional help.

Mention has been made of only a few who contributed to the production of this book, and there will always remain many of whom we are not aware and who may not themselves be aware of how they have helped.

One name that must be recorded is that of Dr. John Gibson, until 1972 the Medical Superintendent of St. Lawrence's, who constantly encouraged the group to continue with their work and who often watched it in progress.

Special thanks are due, too, to Mrs. Avril Hinkly, the Director of Voluntary Services, and to Mr. Robert Brook, the hospital photographer who is responsible for the illustrations in this book. Finally our thanks go to Mrs. Victoria Shennan for her constant enthusiasm, encouragement, and advice.

GEOFFREY HARRIS
Consultant Psychiatrist
St. Lawrence's Hospital
Caterham, Surrey
England

(The Dr. Harris referred to on page 15 and subsequently is not Dr. Geoffrey Harris who has written this introduction.)

Part 1

MAY THE TWENTY-FOURTH NINETEEN TWENTY

OTTINGDON STREET,
WOLLING ROAD,
CAMBER WELL.

This is where my life begibs. After I was born, my mother was in bed, my Grandma Brewer heard a knock on the door abd when she opened the door, it was my Dad coming home from the army. Grandma Brewer called to her daughter my mother to tell her that her husband had come home from the army.

Part 2

And my mum felldown the stairs before I was born. When I was one year old my mum put me on the kitchen floor, and I used to roll all over the place. Six months after my Dad bought me a chair with table and you could alter it, low or high, and when my mum put my chair low I used to kick the buds out of the garden. Six months after I was two years old.

The original typescript is divided throughout as shown above. Each section of four to six lines represents one day's work by the team.

Joey lives in his wheelchair, surrounded by the personal possessions which make this corner of the hospital "home" to the four friends. Joey and Ernie travel about the grounds propelled by Tom and Michael. Ernie can manage very short distances, having been taught to walk by Tom at the age of sixteen after crawling all the previous years of his life. The four men are a family and have refused any move which involves the break-up of their group, intact for over a quarter of a century. They share the working day and their recreations, and each contributes to the quality of life they enjoy as a united family.

Joey is unable to use his hands in any co-ordinated move-ment. Other res-idents can assist him if Tom and Ernie are otherwise engaged.

From left to right: Tom, Ernie, Joey, and Michael at work.

Leisure activities include appreciation of music and paintings. Work such as simple assembly for commercial firms is also carried out by the team.

MAY THE TWENTY-FOURTH, NINETEEN-TWENTY, OTTINGTON Street, Wolling Road, Camberwell. This is where my life began. After I was born, my mother was in bed, my Grandma Brewer heard a knock on the door and when she opened the door it was my Dad coming home from the army. Grandma Brewer called to her daughter, my mother, to tell her that her husband had come home from the army.

And my Mum fell down the stairs before I was born. When I was one year old my Mum put me on the kitchen floor, and I used to roll all over the place. Six months after, my Dad bought me a chair with table and you could alter it, low or high, and when my Mum put my chair low I used to kick the buds out of the garden. Six months after, I was two years old.

Granddad Brewer got me a tub with sand in it, and at that time my brother Peter was born, and when I was three years old my Mum took me up to Camberwell Park and she took me by the Bandstand, on the swings. When I was about four years old my life in hospital started. The first hospital I went to was St. Childes, and they operated on the backs of my legs. The operation wasn't successful. I went to the hospital in 1924.

One year passed. My school days began, and I did not

last very long. I used to go to school at Otting Street. They turned me down because of my nerves. I could not talk. I was at school for three months. At that time I had a baby sister, Gladys. When I left school I stopped at home, and every morning my Mum used to put me outside the front door. She used to ask me how many motors had passed and I used to answer by blinking my eyes. I blinked once for every motor that passed. My Mum understood this.

My mother and father took me to Southend for a holiday, and I went on a boat called the *Golden Eagle*. I went up the river and up to Tower Bridge. There was a big storm, and my brother Peter and I were dressed in navy suits, and I wore a peak cap. The following year my mother's life ended when I was six years old. That was in 1926.

My Auntie Em took me over, and Grandma Deacon looked after me for a little while. And my auntie had a lot of work to do. She took me and my sister and my brother over. When her daughter Annie grew up, she took Peter and I to Hyde Park with Aunt Nell to see the Horse Guards. And she took me round to Grandma Deacon's home; Grandma Deacon was my Dad's mother. She was a good grandmother to me. At seven years old, I went to Carshalton Hospital for more treatment. They could not understand me when I went to the toilet. I did not like it there and I was at Carshalton for six months.

Carshalton sent me away to Roehampton, Queen Mary's Hospital, for more treatment, and the nurses here were very good to me. And every Sunday afternoon the nurses used to put me on the balcony to look around. My

Daddy, Auntie and Grandma came to see me. On 12th February, 1928, my Dad told me that I was coming to Caterham. On the following Thursday, 16th February, I came to Caterham. I was first nursed on the female ward. I was brought to the male side of the hospital later.

Nurse Dolley French was my first nurse. After that Ruth Boment, and Nurse Dora Bailey. They were all very good to me. I was in a cot and they fed me with milk and semi-solid diet. I was in bed all day. On my second day in hospital, I was examined by Doctor Harris.

On the first Saturday, I got up from bed. My first friends were Cassan Over and Arthur Parsons. They tried to speak to me, but I could not answer them. They were told later that I cannot talk. I was not so nervous at that time. The boys soon knew me. Arthur fed me during breakfast with bread and milk. At dinner time I was fed with bread, beef tea, and rice pudding. For tea I was fed with bread and milk all by Arthur.

On the Monday I was taken to the psychologist and I was asked the difference between triangle, oval shape, and round ring. They were on paper. I pointed the figures with my nose and I got them all right. Also she asked me how many pennies in a shilling. I answered by blinking my eyes twelve times. She understood and was very pleased with me. And this is how I made the psychologist understand me. I went back to the ward pleased with myself. One week after I came to Caterham I settled down with the nurses and the other patients. The following week I had my first visit from Dad. My Dad asked Dr. Harris how much I knew, and the doctor told him I was a very intelligent boy.

[15]

A month went by. May 24th, my birthday, and when I woke up I was trying to tell the nurses and the boys that it was my birthday but they could not understand me. I tried very hard but I could not make them understand me all morning. After dinner Nurse French said she knew what I was saying, as she brought out a lot of birthday cards for me. This cheered me up a lot after the battle to make them understand me. And on that Sunday Grandma Deacon and Aunt Nell came to see me. They brought me a birthday cake which had eight candles on it, and Nurse Dolley asked me how old I was, and I blinked eight with my eyes to answer. June came, and the nurses used to put me on the court in a deck chair. It was nice and hot. Cassan Over and Arthur talked to me. They talked to me about Sports Day, and the Sports Day came round.

It was a poor Sports Day as there was no roundabout and it was raining all day. It got a bit exciting after tea. They got a lorry and gave all the cripples a ride to Purley and back. Nurse Dora Bailey had me on her lap during the ride and one of my boots came off in the lorry. They found that one of my boots was missing in the ward. Nurse Dolley asked me where it was but I could not tell her. The next day the driver of the lorry brought the missing boot back and Nurse Dolley wasn't cross with me. It was not new, anyway.

The nurses still used to put me on the court in my deck chair. I saw planes fly past and this was all I could do, and I was happy. In October I went to the pictures at the R.H., and it was silent pictures in those days. Mr. Stephen used to work the projector while Mr. Bill Ray played the piano. We used to go every fortnight to watch these pictures. My first Christmas here came round. Nurse Dolley put up the decorations. The nurses made lemons and oranges out of the paper for the decorations. My Dad brought a big box of chocolates for us all. My Grandma also brought me a Christmas stocking. I could not thank them for these Christmas gifts. We entered 1929.

We had a new nurse called Violet Morley in our ward. She fed me with rhubarb pudding and all the boys made me laugh. And when I laughed I spat all the rhubarb over Vie's apron, but she wasn't cross with me. I would not have blamed her if she was cross with me, she only put on a new apron. I could not apologize to her as I cannot talk. Nurse Violet is still working in the card factory.

In February this year a schoolteacher called Mrs. Pemilton came into our ward. She talked to me, but I could not answer her. She showed me some photo cards and she asked me to match them. I matched them with the help of a boy who was my friend Arthur. Arthur wasn't sure how to do this thing. I showed him by using my nose to direct him which card to pick and where to place it. The following Monday, Mrs. Pemilton took me out in my chair and walked me round the ward. One thing I wanted to do was to learn how to tell the time on a clock or watch. Mrs. Pemilton asked me whether I wanted to learn to tell the time.

The year went by and we entered 1930. One day Arthur was going to feed me with my sop but I did not want it. Arthur did not know what was wrong with me. He put my sop on the table and had his own breakfast. He tried me with a bit of bread and said to the nurses that was what I wanted. I thought to myself that I would be all right with an ordinary meal.

On the Sunday that followed I had a visit from my Dad. My Dad brought a new woman with him and said to me: "Joey, I've brought your new mother down to see you." The woman was my stepmother. She was very nice to me, just like my real mother. She came to see me every month. It wasn't long before I had a stepsister, her name was Sylvia. My Dad brought my stepsister down to see me. She was two years old and I was thirteen at the time. My Dad took a photograph of me with sister Sylvia on my lap and my brother Peter at my side when I was twelve years old. My stepmother wasn't a very healthy woman. In 1931 she passed away. The marriage did not last long. They put Sylvia in an orphan's home as there was no one to look after her.

In October 1935 my father got married again to a lady from Crystal Palace in a place called Norwood. I only saw her once as she wasn't as good as my other two mothers. I have another stepsister which I have not seen in my whole life. Three months after Cassan Over was transferred to the male side of the hospital. Cassan was the only one that could understand me well. It was a battle when I tried to say something like I wanted to go to the toilet. When Nurse Mary Argo brought a chamber into the ward for one of the boys I made a noise and she understood what I wanted. So she went and brought me one also. On my fifteenth birthday I went along and I started school in the hospital school. Miss Baker was my schoolteacher. I was taught the alphabet and some history. I got better and better. All I wanted to do was talk. I used to think to myself a day will come when I will be able to talk. My sixteenth birthday came round. On my sixteenth birthday my father asked me what gift I wanted from him. I pointed to my wrist and he understood that I would like a watch. On the 4th June I got the watch.

A week later I got transferred to the male side, but only after Mrs. Brain asked me if I would like to go and I had time to think about it. Finally I decided to come over to the male side. I was growing and getting too big for the female nursing staff to see to me. I came to the male side on a Tuesday and soon mixed with my old friends once again. For a time I missed all the female nurses who had been so good to me. I particularly missed Nurse Nora Ovaltine; she was one of the best and my favorite. It was Mr. Davies who brought me over to the male side where I was put to bed and fed by the male nurses. The very next day they got me out of bed. I tried to make Mr. Davies understand that I wanted Arthur to feed me as I was more used to him. There was a cricket match and they took me out to watch it being played. The match took place on the Saturday. It reminded me of how my father used to take me to watch him play in the year 1925. September that year I started working in the mat shop. I have now worked in the same shop for sixteen years. It was the first time I had used my hands when Mr. Teece wanted a special color and I picked one out for him. When I told my father that I had started work he was very pleased. In October 1936 I went out on the field to see a football match, and it was since that time that I became interested in football. The late Mr. Knight scored two goals for the hospital team. The next day when my father came to visit me I started kicking out my legs to show him that I had been watching a football match.

One day in November, I was stood up behind a wheel-chair with my hands on the handles, Mr. Hedley sat in the chair to control the wheels, and they made me walk up and down. I did this exercise for one year, in 1938. When my Grandma visited me I was told that Dad was ill again. On my eighteenth birthday he came to see me, and again in August, but that was the last I saw of him. In 1939 my father's life ended, and he would suffer no more pain.

My brother joined the Territorial Army, and at Whit-sun he and my auntie, cousin, and Ernie all came to see me. My brother looked very smart in his uniform; he was stationed at Dorset and came to see me whenever he was on leave. A short while later, Mrs. Laing left us to take up an important post, looking after wounded soldiers. My brother visited me as usual at Christmas 1939, and I wished him the very best of luck. My cousin Ernie joined the army, he was my cousin Annie's husband.

He joined the Royal Artillery. He was sent to the Middle East. Cousin Annie came to see me the following week and I told her that she should not worry—her husband would soon be back home. After three months Ernie sent me a card and I got my charge nurse to send him one back. I explained to Arthur and Harold Sparks what I wanted to say, and they told him. It took half an hour before they really understood me. My aunt came to see me on my twentieth birthday which was 1940. She was very good to me. She never lets me down. During the air raids Annie came to see me. In September 1940 she told me she was going to join the A.T.S. in Cambridgeshire. She joined and sent me a photo of herself in uniform. I still have it. In November 1940 I had a strange letter. It was from Sutton. I don't know who wrote it. Mr. Fane, my charge nurse, read it.

It was from two girls whom I did not know, one was Josephine. In August 1940 Peter came on leave. He came and brought a nice surprise, my sister Gladys whom I had not seen since I was two years old. I was very pleased. Gladys was brought up by my mother's friends who live at Elephant and Castle in Harold Road. One day I had a letter from Gladys. The other girl I mentioned that wrote to me was Catherine. I wondered how they knew me. Then I remembered Peter told me about them. I asked my charge nurse to write to them for me. By the help of Harold Sparks, I made Mr. Fane understand that I wanted the girls to send a photo. I got it the following week and it was very nice. The girls came to see me three weeks later. They tried to speak to me but I could not answer. My friends told the girls I could not speak. They said they knew, my brother had told them. They were very nice to me. I showed them the picture of Mum and Dad. They said Dad was a nice man. I thought in a way Dad was lucky he got married.

I was still working in the mat shop and in 1941 Mr. Treece got two new boys from the female side. The boys were Ernie and Victor. Mr. Treece asked Ernie to help me sort out the wool. When I wanted something or to tell him something I made some noises to make him understand. It was not easy at first but Ernie did not give in. He tried very hard until he began to understand me. Six months later Arthur was taken to Male Ward A1 because he had bronchitis. I was with Harold Sparks but he took a long time to understand me. My aunt and Grandma came to see me in February 1942. When Ernie was transferred to the male side and came in to me I tried to say hello to him. I tried three times before he understood. Then he said "Hello, Joey." I told Ernie that Arthur had gone to Male War A1 with bronchitis. The Sunday that followed Ernie's arrival, my cousin Ann and her friend came to see me. Harold also had a visit that day. I wanted to talk to my cousin Annie but it was very difficult; Arthur was in A1, Harold had a visit. There was nobody who could understand me. I made signs and pointed to Ernie. Mr. Harris understood me and brought Ernie and I introduced him to my cousin. He understood me. That's how it all began. This was the first time I started to talk a little. We asked her how she liked the A.T.S. I was twenty-two at that time. My cousin was very pleased that she could understand me. Ernie was very good. When she went home she told Grandma how she was able to speak to me through Ernie. In May my brother returned from the army. He came to see me. I called Ernie, who crawled on the floor and Peter picked him up and sat him on the chair. I introduced them to each other and Ernie repeated to Peter everything I said. Peter did not believe anybody could understand me.

I had a letter from Sylvia, who was still in the orphan-age and was in the Girl Guides. She did not stay in the orphans' home. My aunt brought her to see me and I was very pleased to see her. When it was nearly Christmas I had an airmail from Ernie, my cousin, telling me he would not be long before coming home. The charge nurse answered this letter for me; I told Ernie all I wanted to say and he told the charge nurse.

I wrote back and told Ernie that Annie missed him (that was his wife). I told Ernie to keep up the good work in the army. I told Ernie I wished I could help him instead of sitting in a chair all day, and that I was 21 and helpless. I said my prayers to help Ernie. I had a letter from Aunt Nell, and Grandma came to see me and told me in a letter that my sister had got a boy friend in the Fleet Air Arm. My sister Gladys got engaged to him. A year after the engagement, my sister was taken ill in the Sanitorium Hospital. I guess that she had the same illness as the rest of the family. Three months later my brother Peter came down to see me. My sister Gladys passed away and that was how one more member of my family went. The following year, that was 1942, I had a letter from Sylvia. She wanted to know where Peter was. At that time, Peter was due to come home on leave. When Peter came to see me during his leave I pointed to my case under my chair where I always put it. Peter opened the case and I pointed to the letter that Sylvia sent to me. Sylvia said in her letter that she was too big to stop in the orphan's home. Peter told me that he was going to see Sylvia. Peter brought her home. He brought her down to see me with Aunt Nell as well. One Sunday my friend Ernie was waiting for his Mum and sister to visit him. While Ernie was still waiting for his visitors my sister sat by him and Sylvia turned round to my Grandma and said, "Ernie is a nice boy." My Grandma said, "Sylvia, you are making an early start." My sister worked in a sweet shop before she started nursing. I was very proud of her.

The nurses were good and we don't know what we should do without them. 1943 came round and it was not a good year for me. On Good Friday morning I got out of bed with a pain at one side of my neck. I did not complain about the pain the whole day, hoping it would go away, but the next day it was worse. I told my friend Arthur to tell Mr. Fane, the charge nurse, about it. He could not see what was wrong so he put me back to bed and called the doctor. It was Dr. Crawford.

On Easter Monday, my brother came to see me. With him came a nice blonde girl. The charge nurse pushed my bed into the dayroom for this visit. My brother asked me what was wrong. He took my hand out of bed and I pointed to my neck. Peter understood that and he saw a red mark on my neck. He told Mr. Fane, the charge nurse, it was hurting me, and Mr. Fane said he would let the doctor look at it in the morning. I was very restless that night; it was very painful. The next morning I could not move my neck and I got worried because I could not eat anything. Dr. Crawford came up the dormitory and I thought to myself, "I am very pleased to see you." He looked at my neck and said that it was an abscess developing and I had better go to A1.

I looked around to see if anybody there could talk for me but they were all at work, so I took a chance to see if Dr. Crawford could understand me. I nodded my head a little and as luck would have it he knew that I understood. So after dinner they brought a stretcher to my bed and I thought to myself, "This is it, if I want to get better I will have to go to A1." Mr. Fane and Mr. Ayliffe took me there and handed me over to Charge Nurse Sylvester and Student Nurse Griffiths, who said, "Hello, Joey, we are going to get you better."

They put a mag. sulph. paste dressing on my neck and the pain was a bit easier. But it was not easier for long. On Wednesday morning Mr. Griffiths fed me my soup break-fast and asked me how I was, and I pulled a face to make a sign to say I was not feeling too good. He said "Never mind, I will change the dressing after breakfast and it will feel easier." At dinner time he fed me with beef tea and bread. At half past two I heard footsteps coming up the ward—it was my brother with one of the nurses. He said, "You are in good hands now and you will soon be better." Four days went past and I was still in pain. The nurses were still changing the dressing regularly.

The 3rd May came round and it was Cup Final day, be-tween Arsenal and Blackpool. Blackpool won 2–1. The next day I had another visit from my brother and he said to me, "I have got some good news for you. Joey, you will be out of pain tomorrow." I was very pleased. The next morning Dr. Crawford came up the ward and said to me, "Well, Joey, I suppose Peter told you the good news," and I smiled at him to make him understand I knew.

[25]

After dinner Mr. Griffiths got me ready for the theatre and gave me an injection; he and Mr. Goodson took me over there. On the way I saw Nurse Dolley French who wished me luck. In the theatre the surgeon said to me, "I see you have a pain in your neck," and I nodded my head. He said, "Don't worry, we will soon stop it." They put me on the operating table and Dr. Crawford said, "You look nervous," and I thought to myself, hurry up and get it over with.

The next minute they put a mask on my face and in seconds I was away. What the surgeon was doing in that time I was not bothered about as long as I was out of pain. When I woke up I found myself back in bed, with my brother Peter and Staff Nurse Saunders, who was on night duty, standing there. I pointed to the jug on my locker and they gave me a drink. I called them often that night—I must have drunk a gallon. The next morning I was a different boy. I was feeling as right as rain. Mr. Griffiths put a pillow under my head and I was a different boy. Although I was not back to normal I was getting stronger every day. On the following Thursday Mr. Sylvester took the stitches out, and the first breakfast I had was a boiled egg and three slices of bread, and some porridge. Mr. Griffiths fed me, and I thought to myself, isn't it nice to eat once again. Dr. Crawford came to see me and told me that my neck was completely better and that he would not be seeing me again as he was joining the Merchant Navy and the new doctor was Dr. Engler.

My Grandma and my auntie and cousin came to see me on the 23rd, and on the next day it was my birthday. I was twenty-three and Mr. Sandiford, a staff nurse, brought me a big bundle of birthday cards. Dr. Engler came in the ward and asked me how I was. I put my thumb up and he looked at my wound and said that it was healing nicely. I pointed to C1, my own ward, hoping he would understand that I wanted to go back there, but he did not.

So I tried another way. I pointed to one of my envelopes from my birthday cards and he saw it was addressed to C1. He asked me if I wanted to go back, and I nodded my head for yes. He said I was not to get impatient and get up slowly, a few hours each day. "You have had a nasty operation and must not rush things." The next morning I heard the news on the wireless that the Royal Air Force had bombed a big dam. I thought to myself, that is good, the war will soon be over now.

Once again the next morning, Dr. Engler came in to see me and asked how I was. Again I gave him my thumbs up sign. He asked me if I wanted to get up half a day, and I nodded for "Yes, please." Mr. Griffiths got me up in a chair and put a blanket around me. It felt very strange for me to be out of bed and out of pain. After tea I was put back in bed again and I must have been a bit excited because I was running a temperature.

On Friday morning, during his rounds, Dr. Engler said that I could go back to C1. Before I went I said thank you to the doctor and nurses of A1. A nurse took me in my wheelchair to C1 and I was very pleased to see all my old friends again. Seven months went past, and on the 9th November my brother Peter and his girl friend came to see me. He said I was looking a lot better now, and I replied that I had never felt so better in all my life.

I nodded to his girl friend, Pat, who I had seen earlier in the year at Easter. Peter said to me, "In forty-eight hours from now she will be your sister-in-law." I kissed both her hands and congratulated them. I said to Peter, "You are a very lucky boy." On the 11th November they were married in a Registry Office and on the very next day Peter had to go back from leave. The following week I had a letter with a photograph of all my relations and of my sister-in-law's family, too.

I have still got the photograph. My sister-in-law was a ballet dancer. She used to dance in concerts for the troops during the war. That was how my brother met her. That was his lucky day. I wish that I was lucky like him but still, that is how it goes. In January 1944 I had a letter from Peter telling me that I could expect to be an uncle very shortly. I wrote back telling him that I hoped it would be a boy. It arrived a week early, on the 17th May, and it was a boy.

That was another Deacon in the world. They decided to call him Peter after his father. One week after Peter was born my sister Sylvia and my Aunt Nell came to see me and my sister said to me, "Well, Joey, you are an uncle now." I turned round to Ernie and asked him to tell Sylvia that she must be an auntie. She seemed very proud. I asked her how she was getting on with her nursing, and she said she was liking it very much. I asked Ernie to tell her that it was the best job going in the world. I ought to know, as I have spent most of my life with them.

Another week went past, and on the 6th of June I heard on the wireless that the soldiers were landing in France. I thought to myself, we are on the way to victory. Six weeks later one of my lady friends came to see me and tell me that she was getting married. That was a big blow, because I liked her very much. Whoever she was marrying was a very lucky boy. I only wished it was me.

The following year, 1945, when the war ended and the soldiers were demobbed, was a lucky year for me, although it nearly was not. It happened like this. I very much wanted to go home for Christmas as I had never been home for Christmas before. I had been talking to Peter about this and he said it would be alright. Just before Christmas I asked Harold Sparks, another patient, to ask Dr. Lindsay, the Medical Superintendent, if I could go, but I could not get Harold to understand me. Just as Dr. Lindsay was leaving the workshop Ernie Roberts called him back and said that I wanted to go home for Christmas. He said he thought it would be all right. I was very happy. To think he nearly left without me managing to make him understand. Good old Ernie.

Ernie told Dr. Lindsay that I would like to go home for Christmas. It would be my first Christmas at home for eighteen years. He said I should get my brother Peter to write in and ask. I wrote to Peter asking him to come and see me, which he did. He brought his wife and baby with him, and I told him what Dr. Lindsay had said. Peter said he would have to talk to cousin Annie first about it. Annie agreed, so it was all fixed up for me to spend my first Christmas at home.

On the Saturday before I went home, one of the nurses was shaving me during the evening, when the football results came on the wireless. I was in the hospital pontoon and my team was Arsenal. They needed four goals. When I heard the man say they had won 4–3 I jumped and the nurse cut me. I put my foot out and tried to tell the staff I had won the pontoon. They said I was a lucky so-and-so, and the next day I got the money.

The next day my cousin and uncle came to take me home. They wheeled me down to Caterham Station and when we got there I pointed to my pocket and my cousin asked me what I wanted. I told him my purse with my football winnings was there and I wanted to pay my fare but he said it was all right, he had paid for me. The train came in and I was so excited. They lifted me into the carriage and put my wheelchair in the guard's van.

I pointed to my pocket once more and Ernie got my purse out and it was full of money. I kicked my foot out and one of the people who sat opposite me had a newspaper in his hand. I nodded to it and to my cousin to try and tell him I had won the pontoon. Ernie explained to him and he said it was my lucky year. When the train pulled out of the station I thought to myself, I hope I am not dreaming. We got out at Forest Hill and my cousin wheeled me all the way to Catford.

My cousin Ernie said to me, "Well, Joey, we are home now," and he lifted me out of my chair and carried me upstairs. The first person that I saw was my Grandma, bless her heart. They put me in the armchair by the fire, and the first thing my cousin Annie did for me was to feed me my dinner. It was great. At that moment I was thinking of my friend Ernie back at the hospital. If it had not been for him explaining to the Medical Superintendent I would not be here now with my family.

On Christmas Eve morning they played carols on the wireless, and my cousin Annie fed me with a soft boiled egg for breakfast, and I thought she looked just like my mother did when she used to feed me. I kissed her hand to show her what I was thinking. All through Christmas Eve my relations came to see me. On Christmas morning I woke up and thought isn't it nice to be home for Christmas. Cousin Annie brought me a cup of tea in bed. I thought I was living like a lord. I had chicken and mashed potatoes and brussels sprouts for dinner and a nice Christmas pudding after.

During the afternoon my brother Peter, his wife and son, came round to see me and they sat little Peter on my lap. I thought he looked like his grandfather. I stopped up until twelve o'clock that night. There was one of my family missing, that was Sylvia who was on duty in hospital and could not come. I hoped she helped her patients to have a good time as the nurses do in our hospital. When Peter went home he asked Annie whether he could take me out on Boxing morning.

She said, "O.K., as long as you bring him back by half past one because he has to have his dinner before going back to Caterham." He took me out and asked me where I would like to go. I said I did not mind, just a walk to have a look round. He was very surprised when I asked him to stop outside a house and knock on the door. My Auntie

Nell opened the door, and she was very pleased to see me. My cousin Harold lifted me out of my chair and carried me in.

They made me very welcome, and my auntie played the piano. The time soon went and it was not long before we had to go back home for dinner. We said goodbye and my cousin Harold said he would see me later to take me back to Caterham. I had some rabbit pie for my dinner and we finished off the Christmas pudding afterwards. I thought to myself, all good things must come to an end. While I was waiting to come back my cousin Ernie's mother came in to see me, and while we were talking I saw a watch on the table. I made signs to Ernie asking him if they would like me to take it and get it mended, and they said yes. When we got to Forest Hill station I said to myself, "Goodbye, London," and then I was on the train to Caterham. I enjoyed every moment of my leave, thanks to my friend Ernie Roberts. When we arrived at Caterham my cousin Ernie and Harold pushed me up the big hill. That was a tiring job. I got back to the ward at five o'clock.

The first thing that I did was to see Ernie Roberts to thank him for what he had done. I had bought him a gramophone record as a present which he liked very much. I went to bed that night feeling very tired but happy, and thought that was the best Christmas that I had ever had. I went back to the mat shop the next day and started work. I told all the boys what a nice time I had over the Christmas.

Nineteen-forty-six came round and on a Sunday I had a

visit from my mother's brother, Uncle Claude, who I had not seen since I left Carshalton. He was in the Army Medical Corps and was a captain. I asked Ernie to ask him how my grandma, his mother, was and he said that she had passed away. I was very sorry. I had not seen her for five years. She used to work in Douglas Hospital and was sixty-one when she died. I asked Ernie to tell my uncle that I was very pleased to see him and that I hoped to see him again sometime. He said he was very happy that Ernie could understand me, and would come to see me again.

In February I had a letter from a girl called Josephine telling me that she had got married. I wrote back saying that I was very happy for her and glad that she had married an able-bodied man and not a useless body like mine. In March Sylvia had her first holiday from the hospital in which she worked, and came to see me on the Monday. I thought she looked very tired.

She opened her handbag and took out a locket which she opened. Inside was a photo of brother Peter and myself. I remember it was taken on the ship, the *Golden Eagle*. I was dressed in my sailor's suit. It was a long time ago. I told Ernie to tell her I remember my Mum showing me it before. I asked her how she was getting on with nursing and had she sat her exams yet? She said yes, and they were worse than she had at school.

I told Ernie to tell her that although it was hard work, she should keep it up. I asked her whether Peter had told her that I had gone home for Christmas in 1945 and she said "Yes." She was very sorry that she could not get there as she was on duty. "Never mind," she said, "there will be another time." At the end of May, a week after my twenty-sixth birthday, another Deacon came into the world, a baby boy.

I said to Peter, my brother, "You only want a daughter now and you will be like our father and mother, they had two boys and a girl." A few weeks later it was Sports Day at the hospital, the first one since the war had finished. It was nice to see the roundabouts and swings again after those black days. It was nice to see cricket and football matches again and friendly aeroplanes not dropping bombs any more.

Christmas came round again and I thought to myself, this time last year I went home on leave. On Boxing Day I had a nice surprise. Two visitors came to see me. My cousin Ann and Ernie. I was very pleased to see them. They told me that my dear old Grandma was still alive and still got around like a two-year-old, hopping on and off buses like a young thing. Soon it was 1947.

My cousin Annie came to see me again in the New Year and she said she thought that my speech was getting better. I nodded to my friend Ernie, and asked him to tell her that it was impossible for me to talk any better than I do, and if it was not for him, Ernie, I would not be able to talk with anybody. In March, my brother Peter came to see me without his uniform on. The first time that I had seen him out of uniform in nine years.

He said he was now demobbed, and had bought a house in Ilerdown Road, Bromley. I said I was very pleased for him and that it must be very nice to be out of the army

[34]

and living at home with his wife and family again. He said it was. He asked me what I would like for my birthday, and I thought I would pull his leg so I said that I would like to go home for a day. He said, "One day is no good, you mean eight days." I looked at him as if to say, "Do you really mean it?"

I did not hear any more until the following week when Mr. Hooper came into the mat shop and said to me, "Isn't your brother an early bird," and I said to myself, "What, now?"—and then I remembered about the birthday present. It was only the middle of March and he had written in and asked me home on the 24th of May, weeks and weeks early. The next two months dragged slowly by; it never seemed to stop snowing, it even snowed on my birthday eve. I did not know it snowed in May.

The next day was my birthday and it turned out nice and hot, and Harry Pollard, another one of my friends, and Ernie were asked by student Jeff Sumner to get me ready to go home. I felt very excited and smart. Harry Pollard put too much brilliantine on my hair and as I sat out in the airing court waiting for Peter to arrive it ran down my face and into my eyes. In the afternoon, another student nurse, John Powell, was working with the acting charge nurse, Mr. Mason.

At half past one there was a shout from the ward that my brother had arrived. Mr. Powell pushed my chair up to the office where Peter was waiting. They put me in the car and tied my chair on top, and off we went to Bromley. On the way I saw a white building—it was a leather factory. Peter said to me, "Do you know who used to work there?" I said, "Our father," and pointed to my tie. Peter knew what I meant because my Dad always used to wear a bow tie.

We arrived home just before three o'clock and my sister-in-law was bathing her youngest son, David, while the eldest, Peter, was playing in the garden. He took me into the house and sat me in the armchair and there I was, home once more. My brother Peter worked in a baker's shop, and as he had taken a couple of hours off from work to pick me up, he had to go back again.

When he came home from work at five o'clock he brought me a birthday cake with twenty-seven candles on top. I thought what a good brother I have got. We all had a nice tea party, and at six o'clock I had another surprise. There was a knock on the front door and who should come in but my sister Sylvia who had just come off duty from the hospital. She took her cloak off and came into the sitting room.

Peter lit the candles on the cake and I thought to myself, "You don't know how lucky you are, Joey." I was thinking of my mates back in the hospital, especially Ernie who was responsible for me being home. Peter and David blew out the candles and Peter cut the cake. I made Peter understand that I wanted to take half of the cake back with me for the boys on the ward. It was very tricky. Soon my birthday party was over and Peter carried me up to bed and my sister and my sister-in-law came up to say good-night.

I said to myself, "God bless them all." When I turned

my head over in bed I saw a photograph on the dressing table. It was of my Mum and Dad. I had given it to my Grandma Brewer, who had given it to my Grandma Deacon, and she had given it to my brother Peter. I looked at that photo for a long time that night. I don't know at what time I went to sleep.

The next morning, Whit Sunday, Peter came in to me and said "Good morning," and I turned my head towards the photograph and Peter said, "Yes, that photo has traveled around quite a bit, would you like it back?" I did not know what to say. Peter said, "After all, you are the eldest son and should have it." I said, "Thank you very much," and I still have it. He got me up and washed, shaved and dressed me and carried me down stairs. He cut my bread and butter into fingers and said to Sylvia, "You had better feed our brother."

During the morning Peter said to me, "Do you remember the hot water on the gas stove?" I said, "Yes." When we were two very small children at home Peter pulled the saucepan off of the gas stove and I kicked him out of the way before he was scalded.

Dinner time I had chicken and sprouts, and semolina for sweet. After dinner Peter fell asleep while his wife did the washing up. That afternoon we had lots of visitors who all came into the sitting room to see me.

I was introduced to them all and I gave them a friendly smile. Peter came down from his rest and said to them all, "What do you think of my big brother Joey?" One of the visitors said that if I could walk I would not know which of the girls to marry. I thought to myself, that's right. If I could only walk it would be very nice, but never mind, that's how things worked out.

After the visitors had left, my brother said to me, "I am going to take you out tomorrow," and I nodded my head and I looked at the two children and his wife, and he said, "Yes, we will all go together." We had tea and afterwards Peter got his album out and showed me photographs of our Dad when he used to play football, cricket, boxing and swimming. Swimming in our family was the best sport out. Our Mum used to like tennis. So you see our family was quite a sporting one.

We spent a very happy afternoon looking at the photos. He showed me one of Tower Bridge and I got excited. He said, "I know what you are thinking about, that day we went on the *Golden Eagle* dressed in our navy clothes." I nodded and looked at the sky and at the light and I stamped my foot. He put two and two together and said, "Yes, that's right." There was a thunderstorm that day. The next morning, Whit Monday, I had breakfast in bed and I thought to myself, you did not have this in the army, nor do we have it in my hospital.

After breakfast he washed and dressed me while Pat, his wife, cleaned the house. She shouted upstairs that we had another visitor. It was Aunt Nell. Peter carried me down and put me in the armchair, and said to my auntie, "Here is my big brother himself," and she started laughing and asked him if they were managing me all right, and Peter said, "Of course we are." After dinner Peter put me in my chair, and Pat got the children ready and we all went out up to Bromley Park.

On the way there we saw my sister Sylvia coming off duty in her nursing uniform. She asked us where we were going and we said up to the park. She asked if we wanted a hand to push my chair, but Peter said he could manage, he was sure that she was very tired after being on duty all day, and her dinner would be ready and waiting. So we carried on up to the park and watched the children paddling in the pool. It was a nice Whit Monday, and after a while Peter said, "We had better make our way home," as he had to go to work after dinner. He was a baker and had to make the bread for the next day.

When we got home Sylvia was reading, and Peter said to her, "Have you had your dinner yet," and she said, "No, I am studying." Peter said, "Put your book away, have something. You are off duty now. We don't want you going where the rest of the family have gone." I thought to myself, you are right Peter, we cannot afford to lose any more of us.

After dinner Peter took me into the back garden, and I sat there thinking back to my younger days and the chicken hutch they had next door.

Peter said to me, "Do you remember the chicken our Dad used to have?" and I nodded and did the action of hammering to show him that Dad made the hutch. I also remember the next-door neighbor then asking my Mum if she wanted our photo taken and my Mum said she was too untidy, and our neighbor said, "That does not matter,"

[39]

and so we had it taken with my Dad in his shirtsleeves making the hutch. I've still got that photo, and I smiled at Peter to say, those were the days.

Peter gave me my supper in the garden and his two children were running around and climbing up the apple tree. I thought to myself, I wish I could have done that when I was small, but anyway, I am happy as I am. After supper we went into the house and Sylvia went back to the hospital. She said to me, "I will see you again before you go back." My brother put me to bed again that night, and the next morning he got me up early because he had to go to work. His wife, Pat, washed me and fed me my milk sop at the same time as her own two children.

Then young Peter went off to school, and my sister-in-law did some shopping. She left her younger son with me until she came back, and he was as good as gold. I could not talk to him but I made him laugh by stamping my foot; that was all I could do. When Pat came home she thanked me for looking after him and I thought to myself they are very nice children, and I was proud to be their uncle. At dinner time I had boiled fish and mashed potatoes and Pat fed me with them. After dinner there was a knock on the front door and who should walk in but dear old Grandma.

I got a bit excited when I saw her, and she thanked Pat and Peter for having me home, and Pat said she was pleased to be able to do it. At half past five as Grandma was on her way home she met Peter coming home from work. She said to him, "You are a good brother to Joey," and he said, "That's what brothers are for." David's birthday was also the day I was going back to St. Lawrence's. I wanted to give him a present. I pointed to my pocket with my money in it. Peter understood that I wanted him to take my purse out of my pocket and take some money to buy him a small present, which he did. Peter said to me, "Where do you want to go before I take you back?" That was the 31st May.

I was stumped. I could not find a way to make him understand where I wanted to go. The only way I could think of was as we were passing some shops I would try and point to them. It was not easy as we were going quite fast and there was a lot of traffic on the road. I thought to myself, I hope I'm lucky and I kept my eyes open, and luck was on my side because we pulled up at some traffic lights and there was a shop with some records in the window. I pointed to the shop to make him understand I wanted to buy a record, but I did not have time because the traffic lights changed for us to go so I was unlucky after all. I got back to Caterham at half past six, and Jeff Sumner, who was in charge at the time, gave all my friends a piece of birthday cake. I told my pal Ernie that I tried to buy him a record on the way back but had had no luck, so we decided to write to Peter telling him what record we wanted him to get for Ernie. Four weeks later he came down to see me and brought the record with him.

Peter told me that Sylvia was at home and that she was not feeling very well. He thought that she was studying and working too hard and not eating enough, but the following week I had a letter saying that she was better and had gone back to work. I was very pleased. Six months

[41]

went past and my Aunt Nell came to visit me. She brought another of my uncles to see me. His name was Jack and he worked in the leather factory with my Dad. He used to play cricket. It was the first time that I had seen him since I was a baby.

He and Aunt Nell still come down to see me. Why he took so long to visit me was that he could not understand me. Now that has all changed because of my pal Ernie. I asked him, through Ernie, how his daughters Jacqueline and Masie were getting on, and he was very surprised that Ernie could understand me, but he was very pleased. At Christmas time that year Peter and Grandma came to see me and while they were with me I had another visitor. It was my Uncle Claud.

I asked my brother Peter if he knew who it was at the door, and he didn't know, and I told him it was our mother's brother. Uncle Claud recognized Peter straight away even though he had not seen him for twenty years. He told us about his service in the Army Medical Corps and Peter told us that I would shortly be an uncle for the third time. I told Ernie to tell him that I hoped that this time it would be a daughter and then he and Pat would have the same as our mother and father.

Peter said, "Yes, that would be nice, but not to worry too much. Let's just see what God brings us." Christmas came and went and it was soon 1948. In January Mrs. Laing, our physiotherapist, said to me, "I am going to give you a try at walking," and I thought to myself, that's a good idea; no harm in trying, so I will have a bash. On the following Monday morning Ernie wheeled me over to the physiotherapy department and Mrs. Laing got to work on loosening my muscles. I also had electrical treatment to try and loosen them.

I had tried to walk before back in 1939, but without success, so this time I intended to try very hard and give it all I could. It was at that time that we found an old bagatelle table in the storeroom which nobody used. One of the boys put my chair at the end of the table and I rolled the balls up with the back of my wrist, and Arthur Parsons counted up the score. Soon after this Ernie Roberts and I got two teams together, one of cripples and one of able-bodied patients, and everyone became interested, including the staff, and that's how our game began.

On the 23rd March I had a letter from my brother Peter saying I was an uncle again and that this time it was a baby girl. I jumped for joy and got a letter written straight back telling him that his family was now exactly like our Mum and Dad's. Two boys and one girl. A week later my cousin Annie came to see me. She was very pleased to hear about the new baby, and said that the family was gradually building up. I thought to myself, I wish I could do the same. I told Ernie to tell her I was trying to walk again and she wished me luck. I thought to myself, please God, make me walk.

That year I was twenty-eight and in April my sister Sylvia came to see me unexpectedly and I was not ready. I was working in the mat shop and our charge nurse, Mr. Fane, came over and told me. She looked tired and had lost weight. She had been working very hard in hospital. I asked her how our new niece was getting on and she said that they called her Linda and that she looked like our mother. I was very proud to hear that. My birthday came round, it was Monday that year, and when my friend Ernie took me over to Mrs. Laing she said, "I have got a surprise for you. I am going to take you, Ernie, and Michael for a car ride."

She took us to Ashdown Forest and I remember we saw a windmill. It was a lovely day and the car had its top down and there was a nice breeze. I did not know how to thank her, and when we got back at half past five, she said, "You had better work hard tomorrow for the day off today." The months went by and although I tried I still was not walking. One day Mrs. Laing fitted calipers on my leg and stood me up. She held my hands and I stood on my feet for ten minutes. Then she let go of my hands one at a time, and there I was, standing on my own for the first time ever.

Another Sports Day came round. It was fine and warm. One of the nurses put me on the roundabout. I had never been on one before, and although I was nervous at first I soon got over it and enjoyed it very much. In August my friend Ernie went home for the first time. I felt lost without him because nobody could understand me. Those two weeks he was away seemed like two years, and was I glad when he came back. During October our charge nurse, Mr. Fane, was promoted to Assistant Chief Male Nurse and left the ward to work in the office. I was very sorry to see him go.

We soon had another very good nurse in his place. It was Mr. Knight, who later became our Chief Male Nurse.

In November Mr. Knight asked me if I would like to see a football cup match and I told Ernie to tell him that it was my favorite sport and I would like to see the match. That same month I had a letter from my cousin Annie asking me if I would like to go home again for Christmas. I wrote back and said, "Thank you very much, I would like to be home at Christmas again."

On the 14th December, the then Chief Male Nurse, Mr. Hooper, told me that I had ten days leave at Christmas. The following week, on a Sunday, my friend Ernie dressed me, and at dinner time my other friend, Arthur, fed me my dinner and pudding. Shortly afterwards the phone rang and Mr. Nobby Clarke, who has now retired, answered it. My friend Ernie said, "I bet that's for you, Joey," and he was right. Mr. Clark came out of his office and said, "Are you ready, Joey, your cousin Ernie is here to take you home." I said goodbye to the boys and I was off. My cousin Ernie had brought his brother Bob with him who was a greengrocer. He had his lorry and I went home on that. I thought to myself, what good relations I have got. It was a nice day and we arrived home at half past two. I kissed Bob's hand—that was the only way I could thank him. My dear old Grandma fed me some tea. She told me that my sister Sylvia was sick and I said to myself, that's why I have not had a letter from her for a while. I was a bit worried over her and the next day my cousin Annie wheeled me round to my brother Peter's house. My sister-in-law opened the door and called to Peter, "We have got a visitor."

He came and lifted me out of my chair and carried me

inside. All the children were playing on the floor. He said he thought that I was not looking very well, and I said that I was worried about our sister Sylvia. He said that she was in hospital as a patient, not as a nurse, with tuberculosis. This disease seems to be an enemy of my family. Peter thanked Annie for having me home and gave her a pound note for her to buy me a present with. I thanked him and soon we were on our way back home as we had to be in before my cousin Ernie came home.

On the way home Annie said to me, "I will wheel you up to the golf course tomorrow." I gave her an old-fashioned look, and she smiled and said, "I don't play golf, that's where I work. We can go up and you can meet my boss and I shall ask him for a week off so as I can take you out." The next day we went off to the golf course and had a look around. We also saw the boss and he was very nice and gave Annie a week off of work. On our way back home Annie said, "We will go to the pictures tomorrow."

The next morning Annie went shopping and she said, "I will get you up when I get back." So that morning I had breakfast in bed—hot milk and popcorns. My Grandma fed me. While Grandma was feeding me we heard a noise on the stairs. Was I surprised when who should come in the bedroom but my Auntie Rose and my cousin Brenda. Auntie Rose was my Grandma's youngest daughter and my father's sister. The last time that I saw my auntie was in August 1939. She also gave me a pound for Christmas. I wanted to know how Uncle Ted was but I could not make them understand me. He had a gold tooth but I could not see anything that looked like gold to point at. Then suddenly I saw Grandma's gold wedding ring, and at the same time Annie came back from shopping and I pointed to the ring and my teeth and Annie put two and two together and came up with the right question. I was very happy that they understood, and Aunt Rose said he was very well. When they went home they said they would see me again before I returned to the hospital. Annie got me up and washed, shaved, and dressed me and took me into the front room.

Annie cooked the dinner, we had rabbit pie, and dear old Grandma washed up while Annie tidied me up ready for the pictures. Our next door neighbor carried me down the stairs and put me in my wheelchair. On the way to the pictures my chair started squeaking so Annie pushed me into a butcher's shop and she asked her friend Jack if he could oil it for me. He did this, and after introductions all round we carried on. It was a war film and I enjoyed it very much. The other film was a Laurel and Hardy one, very funny. The cinema attendant was another friend of Annie's called Bill Cook.

Annie asked me if I remembered a Mrs. Murray and I nodded my head, and she said Bill is her son-in-law as he married Mrs. Murray's daughter Winnie. He carried me to a seat. I wanted to sit in the back row so that my head, which I cannot keep still all the time, would not annoy anybody, but they were all full up so I had to sit in the row in front. Annie told the people behind that I was a spastic and they were very nice and did not mind a bit. We were in the cinema for two and a half hours and I enjoyed every minute. We came out at half past five.

On Christmas morning, Ernie got me washed and dressed, and up in my chair by the fire. The first visitor I had was my sister-in-law, Pat. She brought me some Christmas pudding, and said to me, "You must not eat the half-crown inside it." I tried to ask Pat how Peter was but she did not understand me.

Before Pat went home she told me Peter had said he was coming to see me after tea. Pat took out of my mouth what I was going to say, and I thought to myself, I hope Peter has got some good news about Sylvia, if she was back to work, and if she was back in her nurse's uniform.

For my dinner I had baked potatoes, brussels sprouts, and turkey mixed with butter. Who should feed me but my Grandma, like years ago when I was her little boy. Now she was feeding Deacon Junior, and that was me.

Well, I had a nice dinner, and by the time I had eaten the Christmas pudding and found the half-crown, I could not eat any more. After dinner was finished, and the washing up done, several of Annie's neighbors came up to visit her, and one of them was a Scots woman named Betty. She was very nice, and I enjoyed meeting them all.

Tea time came round, and just as we were about to start, I heard footsteps coming up the stairs. Annie said, "I bet that is your kid brother Peter," and it was. When he entered the room, Annie said to him, "Would you like to feed your brother Joey?" and Peter said, "Sure I would." He told me that he had a letter from Sylvia and that she was a bit better, but had to go for a chest X-ray and I thought to myself, I hope that the X-ray comes out all right. Peter and myself were worried about her. Then

Peter told me that he was going to the hospital to visit her, anyway. Annie, her neighbor and Ernie all went out for a drink, at a pub called *The King Alfred*. While Peter and myself stayed in the house, we had a good talk. Peter said, "Isn't Ernie a good cousin?" also that when we had no worries, he would learn to drive, then he could have me at home, forty-eight hours every month. I thought to myself, I hope it comes true. About six o'clock, Aunt Nell, her husband and son, came up to see Peter, and when we told them that all the others had gone out for a drink, they joined us around the fire and we sat talking. Uncle Harold said, "Do you remember me visiting you at Carshalton, pushing you round the court?" I nodded my head, but I also remembered that it was a different story when my Dad came, as he used to put me in a spastic's chair and make me walk round the court. All this took my memory back to 1926, when I was six years old.

When Anne, Ernie, and Grandma came back, Peter, Harold, and Aunt Nell decided it was time to go home, and for the remainder of Christmas Day the rest of us sat there playing cards, right up to midnight. Then Ernie said, "It is time I put you to bed." I was ready for bed, too, as I had got very tired by this time. I was asleep right away. When I woke up it was Boxing Day, and as Annie gave me my breakfast in bed she said to me, "Well, Joey, after ten happy days you have to go back to hospital once again." I thought to myself, all good things must come to an end.

So after breakfast, I was washed, shaved, and got ready to return to the hospital. For dinner that day I had chicken soup, and Ernie's brother Bob was supposed to pick me up at half past two but he did not turn up. When a friend of Ernie's called, in his lorry, he was told what the trouble was and he said to Ernie, "Put him up in the lorry and I will take him to the station at Forest Hill." When we arrived there, Ernie took me under the bridge and into the station, and while he was away getting tickets for the train, some American soldiers came along and started talking to me. I put my thumb up to let them know that I could not talk, and they seemed to know what I meant.

When Ernie came back with the tickets, he told me we had five minutes to wait for the train, and how he got my chair up those stairs to the platform in time I do not know. However, just as we got to the platform, I heard the train coming in and thought to myself, in a moment I will be on my way back to the hospital with my friends. When the train drew in, the driver called to my cousin, "Don't bother to take him out of his chair, put them both in the carriage next to me." Then Ernie said to me, "What are you waiting for? Get up there and drive the train yourself; make yourself useful."

I thought to myself, if only I could make myself useful; if only Someone up above could give me the power to do the things I wanted to do. Then I thought, oh well, you can't have all the luck. As our train went along I looked out of the window, and I thought how nice the countryside looked, what a lovely country England is, and I felt proud that I was born in this land. It seemed in no time at all I was back at the hospital. I had thanked the train driver for the nice ride, and Ernie had all the hard

[50]

work of pushing me up that hill, and we reached the hospital just after five.

Although I enjoyed my holiday, and was happy to be back among my friends, I was still a bit worried about Sylvia, and wondered if she was getting better. I remember that at the time of getting back to my ward, Mr. Knight was in charge, and everyone welcomed me back, but as soon as I met my friend Ernie, I asked him to thank cousin Ernie very much for all he had done for me. Pushing me all that way, he must have been tired out. I expect it reminded him of his time in the Middle East, when he was pushing heavy guns all over the place. Anyway, he is a good man, and I know his wife Annie is proud of him.

Early in 1949, we had to move out of our ward while it was being painted out, and on the 6th January of that year I had a letter with bad news. It was from Peter, and he told me that Sylvia had been taken to the Sanitorium. I was very sorry to hear this. She was halfway through her exams. I said prayers for her every night, praying that the doctors would be able to do something for her. I remembered that Peter's birthday was on the 17th January, so I bought a tie and a birthday card for him. I knew he was more worried than I was. There were three of us in the family, not counting my stepsister Ruth, whom I had never seen in my life.

She was the daughter of my father's third marriage at Crystal Palace. In February I had a letter from Peter telling me that Sylvia was a little better. I wrote back and told him to keep his fingers crossed. In March she had an operation on her lung, and by the end of the month was a lot better. It was early days yet for the doctors to know whether she was properly cured. In April, I had a visit from my cousin Annie, and I asked Ernie to ask her how Sylvia was. She told me that she had seen Peter, and he had told her that she had lost a lot of weight and needed building up a lot.

She was not eating her food well, and instead of resting was still studying hard, she loved nursing so much, yet now she needed a nurse to look after her. I prayed every day she would get well, I did not want any deaths in my family, and she had been such a good stepsister to us. From then on, every time I had a letter from Peter, I was afraid to open it, afraid that it would be bad news. It was about six months later, in July, the weather was warm enough to have our breakfast out in the court, and this morning the staff nurse, Mr. Doyle, brought me a letter from Peter telling me that he would be coming to see me on the following Sunday. When Sunday came round, and Peter walked in the door, the first thing I noticed was that he was wearing a black tie, and a black diamond on his sleeve. He told me that Sylvia had passed away two weeks ago. It wasn't really a surprise to me that bronchial trouble had struck my family once more, but when Peter said, "Well, Joey, we are on our own now," all I could say was, "I don't know what is round the corner."

But then I told Ernie to tell Peter to try not to worry, as we have got good relations, that is one thing, thank God. I asked Peter where our stepmother and stepsister were, but he said he had not seen or heard of them since they were at Crystal Palace, and they must have forgotten us by now. I also told him I still hope to have a nurse in the family, his daughter Linda, and Peter said, "That is a long way off yet, she is only three, but if she follows my side she may be a nurse, yet if she follows her mother she will be a ballet dancer." I thought to myself, nursing is much more important.

As time passed on, I gradually got over the worry of losing Sylvia, and kept myself cheerful. One day I heard that Al Ward had a television set. My friend Ernie was in bed with a bad foot at the time, and I told him that I would like to write to the committee asking for one for our ward. Of course, they all laughed at me for this, and someone even said "You are out of your mind." I thought to myself maybe I am, but anyway I am going to do it. I asked another patient to write the letter for me, and put it in to the committee. The following Saturday I was working in the mat shop when Dr. Engler walked in. He came up to me and said, "I hear you are asking for a television set." I was with another friend of mine at the time, Harold Sparks, who could understand me quite well, and I asked him to tell Dr. Engler that I wrote that letter for all the spastic boys in my ward. Then Dr. Engler said, "Well, I can tell you that there is one on order for you." I did not think any more about it, but later I told Ernie what the doctor had said. We had no idea when we would get it, but it was on the 19th October, on a Tuesday, that Tom Blackburn came into the mat shop and said, "Joey, the television man is here."

I said, "You mean there is a television set here?" Tom said, "Yes." I told Ernie to tell all the boys, and the next minute they were all shaking hands with me, and the boy who asked me if I was out of my mind said, "I take back what I said Joey." I said to Ernie, "Tell him he is really right, because that is what we are all here for." That caused a laugh. When our charge nurse, Mr. Knight, was promoted to the head nurse's office, we were all sorry to see him leave us. Then Mr. Woodward took over the ward, and my thoughts went back twenty years, as when I came to the male side the charge nurse was his uncle, Dick Woodward.

Through Ernie, I had quite a chat to Mr. Woodward about his uncle, and I asked him if he played cricket, and he said, "I am a fast bowler." I said, "I thought I saw you playing against Dartford, and we won the match." Not long after, I had a bad spell. I had a gumboil, and when the charge nurse showed it to Dr. Engler he told me that when it was better I would have to have a tooth out. Well, the gumboil burst, and I had some awful stuff in my mouth, so I had to have a mouth wash.

The following Thursday, Tom Blackburn took me up to A3 Ward, and the tooth was taken out. Afterwards, I saluted to Mr. Pomeroy, trying to thank him. When Tom took me back to the ward, we had tea, and then played housey-housey—I won four shillings. After the game I went to bed, and that was the first good night's sleep I had had for a week, since my tooth started troubling me. It was nice to be free of pain once again. The next Sunday I had a visit from my mother's brother, Uncle Claud.

He was very pleased to see me, and had brought some

[54]

biscuits for me. He asked me how Peter was getting on, and I told him I had not seen him since we lost our step-sister, Sylvia, and although Peter did not say anything, I did not think he looked at all well himself. In 1950, we had a student nurse named Joe Orchard with us, who thought a lot of me, and one day he took myself, Ernie, Tom and Freddy Jackman to the cinema. The picture was called *The Song of India*. It lasted an hour and a half, and I enjoyed every minute of it.

When the film was over, Tom put me in my wheelchair and Freddy pushed me all the way up the hill and back to the hospital. In November of that year, Dr. Firmin, who was the Deputy Medical Superintendent, brought some student nurses around, and two of them were brothers named Atkins. They were studying, and Dr. Firmin asked Ernie how I was. I replied that I was thirty years old last 24th May. When the student nurses left, I said to Ernie, "One of those two brothers will be the charge nurse of our ward in twenty years time," and Ernie said, "How old will you be in twenty years time?"

I said, "You would bring that up. I will be fifty, getting near retiring age." When Christmas came round again, I was visited by my cousin Annie and Grandma. I was pleased to see Grandma still going strong, as she was eighty-two. My cousin was looking very well, too. I asked her how Peter was doing, and she told me that he was quite well, and that he would be down to see me after Christmas.

When Christmas was over, and 1951 came round, I was

seen one day by Mrs. Laing, who told me that she was getting me a spastics chair that could be made high or low, and a table with it.

She said, "Would you like a chair like that, Joey?" I said, "Yes please, I certainly would." When I got the chair, I thought back to my early days, when each time Arthur fed me my chair had to be lowered. One day about six months later, Dr. Engler came to see me, and told me that he had some tablets that would help to relax the muscles and asked me if I would like to try them. I did not like to say yes, as I thought these things must cost the Ministry of Health a lot of money.

I told Ernie to tell Dr. Engler what I was thinking, and he said, "It is nice of you to look at it that way, but if they can help you it will be worth it." When I had been taking the tablets for a week, I felt that my muscles were much more relaxed when anyone started speaking to me.

Then someone asked me what was wrong with my hair, so I told Ernie to ask him why. He said, "Ernie, you have got a blondy friend," so I looked in the washroom mirror, then I said to Ernie, "He is right you know, and you're a blondy, too." Then I said, "I think it is those tablets that have made us go blond." Ernie went and told Mr. Richards, who was our staff nurse at the time, and he came and had a look at me and said, "You are nearly as fair as I am."

I said to Ernie, "Ask him if he thinks it could be the tablets that have made us turn blond" and Mr. Richards said, "You may be right, Joey," and he went and had a look at some of the others that were on the tablets. They were going fair as well, so he told Mr. Woodward about it. When Mr. Woodward saw Dr. Engler, he told him, and he came and said to us, "Don't you want to stay younger?" and Ernie said, "Sure we do, but the tablets are doing the wrong thing." Dr. Engler laughed at that, but after one month we were taken off them.

Four weeks later I was visited by my auntie, and she told me that she was a grandma, and Uncle Harold a granddad, and I was a first great cousin. I asked how my brother Peter was, and Aunt Nell told me that when she last saw him he was not too good, but he was going to write to me soon. Two months went by, and I had a strange letter. The late Mr. Mason read it to me. It was from a Reverend Griffins, in Hastings, and it was to tell me that my brother Peter was admitted to Hastings Hospital.

I thought to myself, what's the matter now, but the letter went on to say that there was nothing to worry about. Still, I thought, I have had enough bad luck in my family, and I don't want to hear any more. A month later I had a birthday card from Peter, and he wrote on it, "Don't worry Joey, I shall be alright. I'm having my operation any time now." He did not tell me what operation he was having, but I could guess what it was as he was in a hospital by the sea.

I got Ernie to ask the charge nurse to write to my sister-in-law saying how sorry I was to hear about Peter, but I never had an answer to that letter and I was ever so worried about him, although I did not let anyone see how worried I was, or so I thought. Another spastic boy like me, named Victor Boyd, was visited by his brother Alan, and he asked Ernie if he would like to go on an outing to Bognor. Ernie said, "Yes please, if Joey can go as well, as he has a lot of worry on his mind."

So to Bognor we went, on the following week. That was my first outing and it cheered me up a lot, as it was a very nice day. I thanked Victor's brother Alan, and he said he was happy to cheer me up. Sports Day came round, and visitors were invited, so I got Ernie to ask the charge nurse to write to my cousin Ernie, asking him if he could come down that day; he answered straight away, that he would be here. On that day, my friend Ernie's Mum and his sister came down, and my cousin and Ernie's sister went on the swings together.

I thought to myself, I wish I could do that. I was too frightened to go on the swings in any case. Anyway, I really enjoyed myself that Sports Day. I was still thinking about Peter, and about a week later I had a letter and a parcel from the Reverend Griffins; there was a Bible in the parcel, and in the letter the Reverend Griffins told me that Peter had had his operation and was getting up for half a day. I knew my worries were not properly over, because one year back my sister Sylvia had a similar operation.

I thought of all this, and I knew that things were in the balance. I asked Ernie to write to the Reverend Griffins, thanking him for letting me know about Peter.

It was about this time that Mr. Bailey came to our ward and one day, when I was working in the mat shop, he sent Tom over to bring me back to the ward; he put me by the fire and told me that Dr. Uloth wanted to see me. I sat there shivering and worrying as to what it was all about.

When my friend Ernie came in from work he said, "You look sad Joey." I said, "Yes, I have lost my brother Peter, and am now on my own, although I still have some good relations." I thought, now my next of kin is my Uncle Jack. That day Ernie tried to get me to go to the circus with him, but I said, "No, you go and enjoy yourself." I did not want to share my worries with anyone else.

On the following week, I had a letter from my dear Aunt Nell, telling me that she would be down on Sunday with dear old Grandma, and this cheered me up once again. The Christmas of that year was not far off when we had a student nurse come to us named Mr. Freestone, and the first time he shaved me he started talking to me, and asked my name; I was looking round for Ernie, as I don't like strangers asking me questions when he is not around. I couldn't expect a student nurse to know that I had to have someone to talk for me. When I saw Ernie later, I asked him to explain to Mr. Freestone, and to tell him my name. He soon got used to us, and he made a very good job of the Christmas decorations—the ward looked very smart. Two weeks before Christmas I was visited by my cousin Annie. She was very good to me, and along with Aunt Nell and Uncle Jack, helped me over my worries.

We spent a very enjoyable Christmas watching television, playing records, and a game of bingo. Soon we were into 1952, and about the middle of January a man came to see me; his name was Barnard, and he told me that he was a speech therapist, and asked me if I would like to speak properly. Ernie told him I would. Then he asked Ernie how he came to understand me, and Ernie told him how it all started. One Thursday Mr. Barnard took Ernie and me to his office, sat me on the table, and asked me whether I went to the pictures.

I told him, through Ernie, "I go every Friday." Then he asked me what picture I would be seeing tomorrow, and I said, *The Red Berets*; it was about the battle of Arnhem, and I had heard that it was a very exciting film." After we had talked for some time, Mr. Barnard suddenly said, "Now I have got a surprise for you." He picked up a tape recorder from under the table and switched it on; and when we heard our voices coming from it we almost jumped out of our skin.

He had been recording our voices all the time, and when I heard it I could not believe my own ears. How Ernie could understand the noises I made, goodness only knows. On the 6th February that year, I heard on the wireless that King George VI had passed away, and I told Ernie that he was the 62nd monarch of England, and the 63rd would be Queen Elizabeth II.

The following week, Ernie took me to the P.T. room with Mrs. Laing, and while we were playing with a ball, Ernie broke his thumb. He was out of action for three weeks, and while he had to stay in the ward I missed him, having to rely on Harold Sparks or Arthur Parsons to understand me. Two months later, in April, I was told by the charge nurse that the new lady psychologist wanted to see me; she had just joined the hospital.

By this time, Ernie's thumb was much better, so I was thankful that he would be able to go with me. I didn't want it to be like the last time I went to the psychologist, when all I could do was to make signs with my eyes and nose. Ernie did take me, and the first thing the psychologist did was to show me a picture, and ask me what was wrong with it; I told her the people were getting on and off the bus in the middle of the road, instead of at the bus stop, and that is wrong. Next, she showed me a picture of two cars, and asked me the difference between them; I had to smile as I told her that one car had round wheels, and the other one square; I also told her that the one with square wheels would never be a success, as the public would never buy it. Then she asked me how many pints I would have in a gallon of petrol; when I answered eight, she said how many in ten? I answered eighty.

The psychologist was very pleased with me, and thanked Ernie for helping her. Then she asked me if I would like to go out for a car ride with Ernie and Tom; I said I would like that very much. The next Saturday, she took us to Croydon in her car and, although it was a wet day, we enjoyed the ride. The following day I was visited by Aunt Nell and Grandma, and I was pleased to be able to tell them that I got all the psychologist's questions right. Aunt Nell said she always knew that Joey was a brainy boy, the intelligent one of the family, and that it was kind of Mrs. Bourne, the psychologist, to take us out for a car ride.

Four days after this we went to the physical training room in the morning, and Mrs. Laing said, "No P.T.

today boys, I am taking you to a party." I thought, "What, this time of day?" Then she told us that it was a farewell party, that she was retiring, and that Mrs. Budd would be taking over from her. Although we enjoyed the party, we were a bit unhappy at the thought of losing Mrs. Laing. She had worked very hard on the spastic boys and we were all sorry to lose her; we thanked her very much for all she had done for us.

Two months went by, and another Sports Day came round; my auntie and grandma were here, together with Ernie's mother and sister, and we all sat under a marquee because it was raining. Grandma was all right; she smoked cigarettes one after another, and I told Ernie to tell her she would get cancer if she wasn't careful. She laughed and said, "I have only got to die once. Besides, if nobody was ever sick, the doctors would be out of work." I said, "You are right there."

The following September, my auntie took us on an outing to Eastbourne. The weather was fine but windy, and we had a very nice time. I sat watching the boats go out, thinking back to my early days when I was taken on board another boat, the *Golden Eagle*.

Anyway, I really enjoyed that day, and when the time came for us to go back to Caterham I was dead tired.

The first week in October, on a Tuesday, I was working in the mat shop when Mr. Bailey came in for me to go back to the ward. He would not tell me what it was for, so what a surprise I had when I saw who had come to see me; it was my Uncle Jack Brewer, the oldest brother on my mother's side. He said, "Hello Joey, aren't you a big boy now?"

He chatted away to me for a long time, taking my memory back to the old days, and I was laughing and nodding my head in answer to him, and wishing that Ernie was there. Suddenly he asked me how Peter was, and I put my hand up to the black tie I was wearing, and Mr. Bailey told him that I had lost my brother and that was why I was pointing to my black tie. My uncle told me that he was very sorry to hear that. Then Mr. Bailey told him that I still had plenty of visitors, and mentioned my other relations. It was strange how as soon as my Uncle Jack walked out of the door to go home, Ernie walked in. I said to him, "I wish you had come in a bit sooner, as I had a visitor here, and could not talk to him." Still, I knew that Ernie could not always be at my side.

I told my cousin Annie how surprised I was to be visited by Uncle Jack Brewer; I thought he had forgotten me. About a month later, my friend Ernie bought some goldfish, and this reminded me of a story about a goldfish, so I mentioned it to Ernie and he said, "All right Joey, let's hear your story." I started telling him of the time, long ago in my early days, when I used to cry every night as soon as my Mum put me in my cot.

We had a goldfish in the house, and when my Mum noticed how it used to amuse me to watch it swimming round and round, she put it on the mantelpiece so that I could see it. That stopped my crying, and got me off to sleep. Ernie said, "That was a nice little story, Joey."

As Christmas drew nearer, the nurses began putting up the decorations once again, and I said to my friend, "This will be our first Christmas to hear a speech by the Queen of England." Nineteen-fifty-three was Coronation year, but earlier in the year we were looking forward to the Cup Final, which we would be seeing on television. When Ernie had asked me who I thought would win, I had told him that I would like to see Stanley Matthews' team win. Cup Final day was very hot. We watched the match on television, and Blackpool beat Bolton three goals to one. It was joyful to watch, and I was very happy at the result.

As Coronation Day drew near, the staff began putting the flags up, and we looked forward to the 2nd June. When it came, we were all given the day off to watch it on the television. It was a lovely sight, and very interesting to listen to the commentator; it all helped my knowledge of the Royal Family a bit more. Soon after this it was Sports Day again, and this time we had a treat—we were entertained by the band of the Coldstream Guards.

My friend Arthur was transferred to F1, the T.B. ward, and I missed him. The first week in August, I asked my auntie if there was any chance of me going home again, and she told me we would have to wait and see. The second week, Ernie went home, and three days later I was watching the test match on television when Mr. Bailey came over to me and said, "I have got some good news for you, you are going home for the weekend, Saturday until Monday." When Saturday came I was too excited to eat my breakfast, and to calm me down a bit Tom had to push me around the court. My cousin came for me at midday, and I was soon in his van and on my way home again. They had kept it a secret from my Grandma, so she got a surprise, but was pleased to see me. I had a very nice weekend but it went quickly, and it seemed in no time at all it was time to return.

I kissed Grandma goodbye, and that was the last time I saw her. She had been very poorly, though she never let anyone see this; she was always so cheerful. I thanked Ernie for having me home, then I was away. We got back to Caterham just in time for dinner, and after I had been fed I asked Michael to push me over to F1 court, where I saw my friend Arthur and told him all about my weekend at home.

While I was talking to Arthur, Mr. Bailey called out to me telling me not to go to work as I had to have my T.A.B. injection. I thought to myself, "There's a nice welcome to come back to."

A week later, Ernie came back from leave, and wasn't I pleased to see him. We told each other all about our time at home. For the rest of the year it was the usual routine, except that we visited F1 quite often to see Arthur. By Christmas, I was glad to see that he was looking much better, thanks to the doctors and nurses. One day, I was watching T.V., and although I did not know it one of the doctors was standing behind me. He stood there for a quarter of an hour before I noticed him, then he told me that he had been studying my nerves and that, for a spastic, I had sat still for a very long time. I told Ernie to tell him that whenever I became interested in anything, such as a good program on the T.V., my nerves always relaxed. It was good to know that the doctors were taking an interest in us.

As our next Sports Day drew near, we were told that this year our wheelchairs had to be decorated; of course, this meant more work for the nurses, but they were very good and sent us out looking very colorful when the day arrived. The Hospital Management Committee inspected us, then gave us all a prize each. In September I went to Worthing again, with Ernie and his relations, as by this time my Grandma needed a lot of looking after, so cousin Annie could not take me out. As Ernie was with me, I was able to talk to people and I said to him, "There must be lots of others like me who would be happy to have you with them, to understand what they say." Ernie said, "Yes, I can imagine what it must be like with no one to talk to." I thought to myself, I am lucky really, as there are many worse off than me; what about the blind, I feel very sorry for them at least I can see what is going on around me.

One day in 1955 I was taken ill with a pain in my neck and a high temperature. When the doctor examined me, he said it was a swollen gland and that I would have to go to A1 and have some penicillin. I went to A1 and the next day I was much better. I thought "That was quick. I have medical research to thank for that."

I was only in A1 for a couple of days, and as I left I smiled my thanks to the nurses for making me better.

After returning to my own ward, I went along to the mat shop the next Monday morning, and the boss told me he wanted a brick colored, rusty red wool. I picked out a boxful for him in a day, and when the Chief Male Nurse came in he said, "Are you sure you have the right color there, Joey?" I said, "You ask the Governor," and he gave me a smile as much as to say, "You cheeky so-and-so." The boss said, "Joey knows his colors all right."

In September, we were treated to a fireworks display, and although it was a lovely sight, I couldn't help thinking that it was money going up in smoke. Still, I suppose if the patients enjoyed it, it was worth it.

Soon it was Christmas again, and Mrs. Laing came to visit us from retirement. She said to me, "Are you walking yet, Joey?" I said, "No, and don't think I ever will now, as I am getting too old; still, it's nice to see you again, all the spastic boys know what you tried to do for them."

Well, another Christmas slipped past, and we were into 1956. By this time, one or two of us had begun to try our luck on the football coupon, and one Saturday in January I came back from a Pantomime, and with Ernie to help, checked my coupon. I said, "I think I have the Three Draws up, you had better check it with one of the nurses." Sure enough I had won, and I said to Ernie, "This is going to be my lucky year."

On 30th March a new Doctor came to us, a Dr. Gibson, and he tried to get me to build some bricks up, but it was impossible. I told him I was sorry to waste his time, but he said, "Don't worry about it, boy, I am just seeing if there is anything we can do for you." After that, I was put on some other tablets to help relax my nerves. On my thirty-sixth birthday, my cousin came to see me, and when he saw a notice up about an outing to the seaside he said, "How would you like to go on that outing, Joey?" I did not need to answer that question, as he could read the answer in my face. In June we went to Worthing, and I felt marvelous just to smell the fresh sea air. I said to Ernie, "If I had the full use of my body, I would be the only sailor in our family; it is the finest life there is, and anyone in the Navy must be a healthy man."

In September, our charge nurse, Mr. Bailey, left and Mr. Judd took his place. Not long after this, in October, the country was struck by Asian flu, and I was one of the victims; Mr. Judd had to give me an injection, and not long afterwards he too went down with it. I felt as if it was my fault, and was sorry to pass it on like that; I realized then, what a big chance doctors and nurses take in their work. I was in bed for five days, and was glad when it was over. At Christmas, I was visited by my cousin Annie, who told me that my Grandma was still very ill.

She was now eighty-four and needed a lot of looking after. In 1957 we were shifted around a bit, our ward had to be painted out, so we were moved to E1 Ward. Then in March Ernie was taken ill, and I was stumped again; still, I had Harold Sparks, he could understand me a bit, and Michael could write my letters for me. This lasted for three weeks, then we were back to normal again. I was looking forward to the Cup Final when our television set broke down. We were down in the dumps at first, but then I had an idea. I said to Ernie, "What about asking if we can go to the Coronation Club to watch it." So Ernie asked the charge nurse, and he spoke to the Chief Male

Nurse about it; he said that would be all right, so we saw the Cup Final after all.

In August of that year, Ernie went home once again, and once more I had to rely on Harold to speak for me; still, I did not expect Ernie to give up his holidays for me. He deserved a break from me now and again, and I hoped that God would reward him for all he had done for me; it would be impossible for me to do so, and the same goes for the doctors and nurses. While Ernie was away, a notice went up to say that there was another outing coming up, and as I had enough money on me, I paid for a seat for myself and him, and when he came back off leave, he had a surprise when I told him. The outing was to Littlehampton and, although we enjoyed it, it was our last break for that year.

Two months later, in December, a mass X-ray unit came to the hospital, and we were told that we all had to be X-rayed. I got a bit bothered over this, knowing how bronchial trouble ran in my family, and I was a bit chesty at the time, but I soon realized that it was best to have a check-up and not let things go. I had my X-ray and thought no more about it, just living in hopes. I didn't let it spoil my Christmas dinner. Three days after Christmas, the charge nurse said to me, "I want your chest X-rayed again, Joey," and now I was properly bothered although I had been expecting it.

After I was X-rayed I heard nothing more until one Thursday; it was the 16th January, 1958, and I was given a bath without anything being said. I knew that something was up—it was as if the staff didn't know how to break the news to me. I looked at Ernie as much as to say, "Are we really going to be parted after all this time?"

Ernie tried to feed me my tea, but I was too worried to eat. Then at five o'clock Mr. Cox came to me and told me that I had a bad cough, and that I needed treatment for my chest; this would mean going to F1 the chest ward. He said, "Say goodbye to your friends Joey, it's only for the time being." When I was taken to F1 Mr. Powell was acting charge nurse, and when he saw me he said, "Hello, Joey, you and I are not strangers, are we?" I remembered that he was a student nurse in C1 eight years ago. He put me to bed and said, "You are in good hands, Joey, it's up to you to help the doctors and nurses as much as you can." I was properly worried. I did not know any of the patients except Arthur Parsons, and I did feel a bit better when he came over to me and said, "Are you following me around?" I pointed to my chest and he said, "Yes, I know; it's a rotten complaint, what most of us are here for."

Later on, I saw another patient that I knew years ago, and I thought I would soon get used to this place. Then I heard someone call my name from the window. It was good old Ernie; I knew he wouldn't let me down, and when I thought that he wasn't very far away anyhow it cheered me up a lot. At tea time the next day the staff cooked fried egg and bacon, and I thought to myself, "What are you worried about Joey, you are in a good ward, getting good food; it is silly to worry." And as the different staff came on duty I was glad to see that none of them were strangers to me.

[70]

Two weeks later, I had my first visit in my new ward—I had to talk to my auntie without Ernie's help. Still, it could have been worse, as Arthur was able to understand me quite well. They had brought me a Bible, which had belonged to my mother, and I thought a lot of that. I still have it today. In my first week there I watched the nurses bringing the medicines around, and they passed me by each time, but on the following Monday Staff Nurse Poegal was giving them out, and he stopped at my bed. He said to me, "Is your name Joey Deacon?" I nodded my head, thinking to myself this is it. He said, "I have got some medicine for you, it's a new one out, and sure to make you better." The medicine tasted bitter, but I knew that I would have to get used to it. I was also put on streptomycin.

In March I had a boil in my ear, and each time a dressing was put on it, the movement of my head made it come off again, but one nurse wasn't going to be beaten and that was Mr. Dermodey. He spent half an hour on it, and it stayed there. The next month I was allowed to go out on the veranda, as it was nice weather, and it cheered me up a lot as Ernie soon spotted me, and came over for a chat, and I could also see the cars and lorries from there and that made a change.

In June I had to have another X-ray, and this was the first time that I had been for an X-ray by ambulance; it was because at this time they were being done at Redhill Hospital. The following months I was told that I could get up for an hour after tea every day. I knew then that I was getting better, and I thought to myself, "So far so good. I must eat well and keep on taking my medicines to beat this disease"; and I felt that I had already won a victory over it. I was still on streptomycin but, three months later, Mr. Lipyeat told me that I was no longer on it, only the medicine. This was another good sign to me, and I was happier still.

One day in December, as I had noticed that all the other boys were allowed up all day, I thought I would ask if I could as well; but the trouble was, how could I make anyone understand? Then I had an idea. When Mr. Henderson came to take my temperature, I knocked my head against the back of the bed so that the clothes hanger rattled, then moved my eyes backwards and forwards from him to the hanger; he said, "Clothes?" and I nodded my head, saying "Up" as best as I could.

He understood, and he told me that he would ask Dr. Dutton the next morning. When he came the next day, Mr. Henderson told him how I had made him understand what I wanted, and the doctor said, "Well, that deserves a prize, but for a time you must only get up for every afternoon." I was satisfied with that. Now it was Christmas Day again, and as this is the day that all the patients are allowed to go visiting around the other wards, I could expect to see Ernie; when he came, he was pleased to see me looking happier.

In March 1959, I was sitting out on the veranda one day when some workmen went into the orchard opposite to my ward, and started digging the trees up; I managed to make one of the staff understand that I was wondering why they were tearing the orchard up, and he told me that they were going to build a training center for the patients there. I thought to myself, "That's interesting, I wonder if there will be a chance for me there."

Two months later, in May, I was allowed up all day, but I was told not to get too excited, or I would put myself back where I started; after all, I was still on medicines, and still having my temperature taken every four hours. It was good to get out in the court once again, and I was feeling pleased with myself; I was out every day, and two months later, getting near Sports Day, Mr. Henderson asked me if I would like to go out on the field for that day; I nodded, and he said he would ask the doctor about it. The doctor gave his permission, and one of the staff took a lot of trouble in decorating my chair; I went to the wheelchair parade all dressed up like an Indian chief.

Not long afterwards, in September, I went on a coach tour of the countryside; this was more than I expected, with all I had had, and everyone was so good to me. One day Mr. Lipyeat said to me, "Do you want a job?" I nodded, and he said, "Can you count?" Again I nodded, so he said, "You can have the job of counting the socks for the laundry every week." I did the counting, and made it forty-two, but the tricky part would be how to tell him. I had it all worked out by the time Arthur came along, and he said to Mr. Lipyeat, "Joey says there are as many socks there, as there are panes of glass in those two windows." The charge said, "Well, there are twenty-one in one, so that must make forty-two." I nodded my head, and he said, "You are an intelligent boy, Joey, the job is yours." I thought to myself, "I would like to be able to do much more for you."

On Christmas Day, to our surprise, Arthur and I were

told that we could visit our old ward, C1. Ernie got a shock to see me come in the ward, and when he said, "How did you get here?" I said, "On my four wheels and the boy behind." He said, "You're getting too cheeky since you have been in F1." I enjoyed that day, and was feeling quite happy when I returned to my own ward. Soon it was 1960, and in March I was taken for another X-ray, but it was unsuccessful as I couldn't keep still, so I would have to go again the next week. The next time, I was given a tablet to ease my nerves, and the X-ray was done. The following week, the charge nurse told me that there was improvement every time I was X-rayed, and that I was gaining ground all the time. I thought, "I am winning this battle, the battle that my family did not win." Later that year, I was given a red badge, which meant that I was allowed to go to the field each day, and when my auntie and uncle came in October, I had to get them to fetch Ernie to explain about the red badge. That Christmas made my third year in F1 and the staff gave me a drink of stout; I had never tasted it before.

Nineteen-sixty-one was a good year for me; in March, Ernie came over to tell me that he had asked about me going back to work in the mat shop, and was told that I could. When I first went back, I was put on a different job; it was loom work, and I had to work the pedals. Once I got used to it, I enjoyed doing this work, although it was a bit tricky at first.

In April I was X-rayed again, and about three weeks later I was waiting for my medicine one day, with my feeding cup, and the staff nurse said to me, "You can put that away Joey, because you are off medicine now, your X-ray is clear." I had always had a feeling that the world had a grudge against me, the way I was born, but winning that battle gave me a lot of satisfaction, and I was very grateful to the people who made it possible; the doctors and nurses.

That Sports Day I had the pleasure of telling my auntie and uncle that I was clear; they were very pleased to hear it.

In September we went to the Training Center for the first time; it was a nice place to work in, I was still working my loom, and getting better at it every day. At Christmas we had a party at the Center, and I was fed by one of the female nurses there. I told her that she was the first female nurse to feed me since my teenage days, back in 1935. One day early in the new year, Mr. Saunders, who was then in charge of the Center, told us that we had to look our best, as we were going to be filmed at work. I said to Ernie, "They are going to make film stars of us now," and Ernie said, "Things are looking up." The filming was done by Dr. Yorke Moore, and was shown later to hospital workers.

I was looking forward to Sports Day this year, as I had made a table runner on my loom work, and had asked for it to be put in the show.

When the day came, we took the runner out to the exhibition marquee, and then went around the fun fair, enjoying ourselves. We had almost forgotten about it by the afternoon, when Mrs. Budd came up to us and said, "Has anyone told you the news?" Ernie said, "No," and she said, "You have won first prize with your table runner." Everyone said how pleased they were, to hear that we had won, and I was very happy especially the next week when my name was in the *Caterham Times*. The following September we were taken for a coach tour of Windsor Castle, it was very interesting, and I enjoyed every minute of it.

Soon after this, we had to move out of the ward so that it could be decorated. We had to go up to the top floor, F3, and I had my first ride in a lift since I was at St. Charles Hospital for an operation. We spent that Christmas in F3, and early in 1963 I began to have a bit of trouble. First of all, I went down with Asian flu; I was in bed for three weeks, then slowly got better. When I was fit to go back to work, I was told that I couldn't go as the lift had broken down; anyway, by the time Ernie had got to know, and climbed the stairs, I had thought of an idea. I said to him, "You see that bread basket over there? You could ask Tom to put me in it, and him and Michael could carry me down the stairs." They all agreed, so I was carried down the stairs in the bread basket; the staff kept an eye on until I was safely at the bottom and put in my chair, then I was off to work.

One day in March, we were taken to the Coronation Club, and shown the film that had been taken of us at work; I could not believe my eyes, seeing myself on the screen. In this year there were some changes of staff; Mr. Lipyeat was promoted to the office, and Mr. Sumner took his place in charge of our ward. Mr. R. Atkins came in as his staff nurse, and on his first day he gave me a haircut. I had a spell in bed, with boils, and once again the nurses did their job. In October we went back to F1, and not long afterwards Mr. Sumner told me that this would be my last Christmas in his ward, that I was going back to my old ward, C1. When I told my auntie on her next visit, she said, "It will be nice to be back among your friends." I thought to myself that is true, the only thing I will miss is the special treats we had in the T.B. ward, such as the milk drinks and eggs; still, you can't have it both ways, I was lucky to have been cured.

Christmas went past, and entered 1964. When I went back to work, I was asked by Nurse Mrs. Whittaker if I would like to work in her shop. I said to Ernie, "What me, working with the girls? Supposing I want to leave the room?" She said, "You can tell Ernie when you want to leave the room."

Anyhow, I agreed, and was put to helping Michael in packing dog biscuits in the shape of doughnuts. About a week after starting there, I noticed another nurse there who I was sure I knew, but couldn't think of her name. I kept staring at her, and she came over and spoke to me, asking my name. Michael told her and she said, "I've heard that name before." It was Nurse Violet Morley, now working in the Training Center. I asked Ernie to ask her if she remembered way back in 1930 and she said, "I remember about that apron."

Christmas came and went, and soon we were into 1965. I started it badly, with toothache, so had to go to see the dentist. Ernie told the dentist which tooth it was, and he said, "All right, I will take that out for you later, under

[77]

general anaesthetic." Then he asked Ernie how he was able to understand me, and he said, "That's what everyone wants to know." Then the dentist said, "Well, you are a clever boy, and if everyone that couldn't speak had a friend like you, they would be a lot happier." The bad tooth was taken out the next Saturday, and I was free of pain once more. I went on a week's holiday in April and although it was cold, I felt it did me a lot of good.

The next thing was Sports Day, and while we were on the field we met Miss Marshall, the Chairwoman of the Hospital Management Committee; she was very friendly, and asked me what I thought of the Flower Show.

I said, "This is the best Sports Day we have had so far, and the Flower Show is marvelous; each year I notice a big change in the hospital, the improvements that are taking place." I told her how much nicer the wards look, and how the patients were dressed better, about the pleasant place we work in, and the good holidays we have by the sea. I hoped she understood that I appreciated everything that was being done for us. She told us that as long as we were happy, that was the main thing and we certainly looked happy.

For some time, the workmen had been busy on a new building, which was to be a new school, and at the start of 1966 we were very surprised to learn that we were going to be visited by royalty. H.R.H. Princess Alexandra was coming to open the new school. When the big day arrived, we went to work as usual, but just before the Princess was due, the staff took us outside and lined us up by the roadside. I was very excited, especially when the Princess waved to us as the cars went past. The following year, another young boy came to our ward and was put in the bed next to mine; he was a spastic, and a type just like myself. His name was Vincent Smallwood, and some time later it was as if he wanted to say something, and I thought by his looks he wanted to go to the toilet; I told Ernie this, and he told one of the staff; I knew I was right when Vincent put his thumb up and smiled at me as if to say "thank you," and I was glad of a chance to help someone like myself.

In November of that year Mr. Judd went to another ward, and we had a new charge nurse, Mr. R. Atkins, and I remembered what I had said twenty years ago, about his being in charge of our ward one day. I started off 1968 with toothache, and Ernie said, "What, again?" Anyway, the doctor saw me and once again I was taken to the dentist; this time he decided to take all my top teeth out. Still, I couldn't chew anyway, so I wasn't bothered about having false teeth. On the 18th May I went on my holiday to Bognor; it was the week of my birthday and Mr. Norton was in charge of the party. I went out on my birthday and when I returned he had a big surprise for me. He and Mrs. McDay, who was in charge of the Hostel, had bought a birthday cake, and there it was, on the table, with four candles on it. I had a lovely party, with everyone wishing me "many happy returns." It made my holiday.

Four months after that holiday was over, Ernie went home on leave and Arthur went to A1 ward. As it was getting near Sports Day again, Freddie and Tom asked me what I wanted my wheelchair decorated as. I had a hard battle to tell my third interpreter, Harold Sparks, what I had in mind; in fact it was Derek Towler who suddenly called out, "I know what he said, he wants to go as Francis Chichester in his boat." Everyone thought it was a good idea, and Mr. Atkins helped to make my chair like the front of a boat. It was very well done and took a lot of time, but when Sports Day came I knew something was going to go wrong. It was a very windy day, and by the time I reached the field all the decoration of my chair had been blown to bits, and *Lively Lady* was a shipwreck. That was not a very good day, as apart from the weather, I wasn't able to talk to anyone. I was glad when Ernie came back from his holiday; I told him what a terrible week it had been.

Five months afterwards we were into 1969, and in February Mr. Knight came to the ward and said, "I have got some good news for you," and he told us that some voluntary workers from The John Fisher School were coming to entertain us. He said, "You will need to pull your socks up, because they will be playing you at bagatelle every week." The following Thursday morning, we were on the veranda as usual, when Mr. Atkins came out and told us to prepare ourselves for a shock. When he told us that Mr. Knight had passed away, I just couldn't believe it, he had been such a good friend to us spastic patients, and was liked by everybody. We were all very sad that day, and when Ernie saw Mr. Bowden, he asked him if he could go to the funeral.

We put our money together and bought a nice wreath.

A few weeks after the funeral Mr. Eaton came as charge nurse in the ward, in place of Mr. Henderson, who had retired.

The John Fisher School boys started coming every Friday, and we took to them straight away; they were very friendly, and I was glad to see how quickly they got used to us. They played us at bagatelle, and were most surprised to see how good we were at it. On the 24th May it was my birthday, and they bought me a present and a birthday cake. They also gave up their time on Sports Day, to push us around the field in our wheelchairs, and this was appreciated very much.

On the 16th October we joined the school, and Mr. Clark, the Headmaster, made us very welcome and told us that we would try to make up for our lost time. I have been going to the school every week since then, and it has certainly improved my education. That Christmas I was invited to a tea party there, and I met some more friends. In November we were told that a bagatelle knock-out competition was being played between the wards, lasting through the winter. We thought we would win this easily as we play it so often. We won the first round all right, and it was February 1970 before it was our turn to play again, in the second round. It was a black day for us, who thought we were the champs, to be beaten by the little boys of E1. I was ashamed of myself; still, that's the way it goes in all sport, and we learned more about this later, when the staff challenged us and we beat them, then they beat us two weeks later. They were good sports, and they taught us how to lose in a sporting manner; they also deserved the highest award for the way they keep the patients happy.

The 24th May came round—half of my life had gone by. What's going to happen to the rest of my life? I did not know. In 1970 it started off all right; my friend Ernie's brother-in-law came to see him at Whitsun. I asked him if he could write to my nephew Peter, who was stationed at Portsmouth. It took a long time to find him—three months in all. The letter went all round Portsmouth. What found him was his name, Petty Officer Deacon; he was the only one with that name in the Navy at that time.

One morning that year, Charge Nurse Eaton brought me a letter and said to me, "I've got a letter from Portsmouth." I turned round to Ernie and said, "Ernie, my nephew Peter got that letter which your brother-in-law sent him." Wasn't I pleased to hear from him. My nephew Peter came to see me with his girl friend Brenda. Wasn't I proud to see him. He brought me a Navy book with his boat in it, also with his photo in it. My nephew Peter said to me, "In 18 months time I'll be getting married," and he asked me if I would like to go to the wedding. I looked at my friend Ernie. Peter said Ernie could come and Tom also. Peter takes me to Carshalton every four weeks. That was a good start and more to come.

Four weeks after, my other nephew came down and I was working in a training center. One Tuesday, at half past ten, my favorite maid, Mrs. Phylis, came down to the training center and told me, "Joey, you've got visitors." She said to me, "There are two boys come to see you." When I got on to the veranda I turned round and said to

Ernie, "That is David and he has eyes like his Grandma, and that is my Mum." And once more I was happy. The second half of my life had started off all right.

My nephew Peter came down on his birthday, the 17th May; also Brenda came down. Peter asked me if I would like to go out on my birthday the following week, the 24th May, and I said to Peter, "Yes, I would." Peter asked the Charge, "Would it be all right if I take Joey out?" And the Charge said, "Yes, I think it would be all right."

The Monday before my birthday the ward got excited. They got a color T.V. I say we have got the best charge nurse in the hospital. And I say the hospital authorities are good.

My fifty-first birthday came round. Ernie and Tom got me ready about 10 o'clock. Peter came down by himself. Peter said to me, "Where do you want to go on your birthday? I think I shall take you to Brighton."

And so on my fifty-first birthday, the 24th May, my nephew took me and Ernie and Tom down to Brighton for the day. It was a nice hot day, and my nephew Peter took me out of the car and put me in a deck chair on the beach. It was the best birthday I'd had since 1947, when his Dad had me home. And we stopped at Brighton till three o'clock.

On the way back to Caterham we stopped at Gatwick Airport. My friend Ernie showed Peter his niece's address and Peter asked Ernie, "Do you want to go and see her?" Ernie said to Peter, "If you've got time." Peter got out his road map and started to study it. So off we went to Carshalton. And that's how my fifty-first birthday finished up. Some more exciting news followed the following week.

On the following Monday my nephew David came down with his children and it made me more excited. It made me feel older than I am, a great-uncle to the three of them. He gave me a photo of his wife Mary, and also his children. Two months went by and my friend Ernie said to me, "How would you like town parole?" I said to Ernie, "It is up to the authorities of the hospital," and I said to Ernie, "It is taking a big risk." And I turned round to Ernie and said, "There is no harm in trying."

I said to Ernie, "This is a free country." Ernie asked the two charge nurses about it. First of all they were not on Ernie's side. They were thinking of the traffic, which they were right to do. Mr. Atkins and Mr. Eaton saw Mr. Bowden. We did not hear any more for three months. Mr. Ryves down at the Training Center took us out to Littlehampton for the day one Friday, and he let Tom, Ernie and me and Michael go down the town by ourselves.

We would not cross until the traffic was clear. Mr. Ryves was watching from the other side of the road, and when we got back to the coach that Friday, I got a good report when we got back to the hospital. On Wednesday Mr. Ryves went to the office; the following week we got our town parole. The first Saturday we went to Dene Hospital Fair. We had a nice time. That was how the second part of my life began. Two more weeks went past.

On a Monday dinner time we were on the veranda. My friend Ernie said to me, "Joey, who's here?" It was my favorite niece Linda. And wasn't I pleased to see her. She brought me a beer mug from where she worked. I showed her all the photos of her grandparents, and I showed her where I go to work. She did not believe I worked. Linda told me her brother was getting married the following year. I told her Peter told me I was going to the wedding.

It will be a great day for Ernie and me and Tom, and I am really looking forward to it. October came round and they sent me for an X-ray because I was a bit chesty. They put me to bed and gave me a sleeping tablet. They are things I don't like. It is very awkward for the spastics, and the doctor ordered me to go to the physiotherapist and Mrs. Morgan, her assistant, and after a while I found my chest getting a bit easier. One evening in October Peter and his girl friend took me and Ernie to Carshalton to see Ernie's niece.

We saw the pond with the lights on it. It was a good night. When I see my brother's children they put new life in me. Once more Christmas came around. The staff got busy putting up the decorations to make the boys very happy. This Christmas we had got a color television. It was the first Christmas program we had seen in color. Three days after Christmas, my niece Linda came down and she brought me a nice pullover.

Ernie told Linda, "It was just what your favorite uncle wants for his chest." And the pullover kept me warm for the rest of the winter. And we come to the end of 1971. That was another good year over. Now we entered 1972. We went to the John Fisher School to see a game of

[85]

rugby. We never saw it because it was so cold, so they took us into the hall to play bagatelle. They beat us one nothing. It wasn't our day at all.

The hospital staff and drivers and the nurses are doing a good job for us. I think to myself that I am in the finest institution in England. I would not like to go away. Everybody is so kind to me, especially the voluntary workers. They come up every Friday to entertain us. What more can we wish for? In March that year Mr. Atkins asked Ernie if we could bring the bagatelle board into the hall. He said that some more spastics were coming up from Croydon.

We played them on the bagatelle board and we beat them two nothing. It was a good game. It was fun to have more spastics like myself to play with. Two months went past; on the 6th April I had an invitation card to the wedding. By that time I was looking forward to the big day very much. In April Mr. Hedditch took us to a hospital called Long Grove in the sunshine coach, to play skittles. I saw some more spastics, worse than myself.

My fifty-second birthday came round. My auntie and uncle took us up to the park, and we had a good talk. The big day came round and this is what happened.

Nineteen-seventy-two, the 10th June. The best day of my life, and it was my proudest day. In the morning I got excited. I got up in my best suit on the wedding day, when my nephew got married, and I waited all the morning for the hour for me to go to the wedding. Two o'clock came round. Mr. Griffin and his wife took me in the car, and Ernie and Tom came with me.

They drove me all the way to Catford and I got excited. We got there at three-thirty and we were the first ones at the church, and Mr. Griffin wheeled me up the aisle. At ten to four Peter came into the church. I am proud to be an uncle to him. Also at ten to four his mother and my niece came into the church.

At five to four the bride's parents came into the church and at four o'clock the choirboys took their place and also the vicar. Also I saw the bride walking down the aisle with her father and three bridesmaids walking up behind them—they were all in pink. And they were my great-nieces. And the service started. The best man was standing behind my chair, and I was proud to be the only uncle on Peter's side.

And there was one more in the Deacon family, and that was what I was thinking all that time. And when the service was over the married couple walked out of the church, and my favorite niece wheeled me out of the church. This was my exciting moment. They took our photo outside the church, of me and Ernie and Tom.

I kissed the bride's hand to wish them all the luck in the world. They put me, Ernie, and Tom in the motor and drove off to the reception hall. When I got there I was surprised to think how many people knew me—Peter's brother, sister, uncle, and aunts on Peter's father's side. My friend Ernie was good to me when he understood me in front of those people, and I don't know what I would do without him. He was so good.

We had drinks, and we had a disc jockey. We stayed there for two hours. You see what a time I had. At seven o'clock we toasted the bride, and Linda fed me with champagne, and at half past seven everybody said goodbye to us. At half past eight we were back in the hospital, and I was dead tired when I got to bed on that day that I will never forget.

Three weeks after the wedding I went on holiday to Dymchurch with Mr. Worthington and three more nurses. We had nice weather but the fourth night we had a thunderstorm and it flooded our bedroom out. Once more the nurses did their job. They must have been so tired after they had finished. They took us to Lydd Airport the following day, and three days after that they took us to Dover, to see the boats coming in and out of the dock. I enjoyed every minute of it.

The next day we went to Hythe. Tom and Michael took us up there. That was one more holiday over. We came back to the hospital brown. In October that year I had a pain in my neck. Dr. Kanavos saw my neck. My friend Ernie asked the doctor what the trouble was. Dr. Kanavos said that I had got arthritis in the neck. He ordered me to go to Redhill Hospital. A student nurse took me in the ambulance.

I saw two doctors at Redhill, and they did X-rays of my neck. It wasn't so easy. I could not keep still. They put me on a narrow table. They still could not take the X-rays. But they never gave up. The doctor had an idea. They put me in a high chair, and strapped me in it. Then they took the X-rays—it was all over in a flash. Wasn't I happy when it was over. They put me in a waiting room, where there were lots of people waiting.

The people tried to talk to me, but I could not talk back to them. The student nurse who went with me told them all about me. I was in the waiting room for one hour, waiting for the driver to take me back to St. Lawrence's, and was I hungry when I got back. Two weeks later I had to go to bed because I had my chest trouble. The following week St. Lawrence's had a letter from Redhill Hospital.

They told Dr. Kanavos there was no cure for arthritis, and I said to myself, "I had better stick it and hope for the best." At Christmas, around the 12th December, Mrs. Hinkly and Nurse Officer Atkins arranged for us spastics to go to Croydon. John Ketcher and two nurses took us. When we got to Croydon we found some voluntary workers waiting to take us round the shops. It was very good of them. They gave us all a cup of tea. When we got back to St. Lawrence's I thanked Mr. Atkins and Mrs. Hinkly for the nice night they gave me. The staff and management are all very good to me. Christmas day came. It was a happy Christmas for me. The two charge nurses were off duty and they gave their time to give the presents out. They were good to do that.

Quarter to eleven Christmas morning I had a nice surprise. My favorite niece and her boyfriend came down. It made my Christmas even more happy. My niece Linda told me that she is getting married on the tenth of March. I asked Linda where she was getting married. She told me it was in Gloucestershire. I told Ernie to tell Linda that Gloucestershire is a long journey. And I told Ernie, "You got a lot of plans when it is a long journey." That was another Christmas over. We entered into 1973. We had a new schoolteacher who took Mr. Riley's place. He is a psychologist. The first week in January I was taken bad with my chest. Once more my friend told Mr. Atkins, and Mr. Atkins shows me to the doctor.

Dr. Kanavos ordered me streptomycin and I could not go to bed. The stuff would lay on my chest if I went to bed. I obeyed the doctor's orders. The doctor understood my position, also the nurses. My friend Ernie is always around when I want him. Ernie is more than gold to me. I don't know what I'd do without him. Sunday at quarter to eleven I was sitting by my bed and my Aunt Nell, Uncle Jack, and Aunt Mary all came to see me. My Uncle Jack had had a letter from the hospital saying that I was ill. When I saw Aunt Mary it made me better. Aunt Mary's son-in-law brought them in his car. I was happy to see them. January went past and we entered February, and we got closer to the wedding. My friend Ernie asked Mr. Davies if we could borrow the hospital transport to go.

The wedding was to take place at Gloucestershire and I told Ernie to tell Mr. Davies that I think it is a long way. Mr. Davies said to me, "I'll see what I can do." Two weeks after I had the good news. Dr. Harris told Ernie the wedding was all laid on. I thought to myself, "Well, Joey, you'd better pull yourself together." I thought to myself I hope my chest is all right by then. The 7th March came round. We went to see Mr. Tippins's next-door neighbor. That was Mrs. Johnson. We went to Merstham. Mr. Peckham took us there. Mrs. Johnson was a nice lady—she mashed up my potatoes. We thank Mr. Davies for that. I wish we could pay him back. Perhaps one day I will. Saturday came and that was the day I was waiting for.

I got up at half past six. One boy called David Harris got my clothes on. I had a bit of catarrh—I knew I had to ignore it just for that day. Anyway I was too excited to eat my breakfast. Tom made me some Complan for my breakfast. I got ready before breakfast and washed and shaved. Time was marching on and eleven o'clock came round. Mr. Peckham brought his station wagon in the court—he put me in the car and Mr. Jenkins, Ernie, and Tom got in and off we went. We went over Hammersmith Bridge and through Oxford and we were on the way to Gloucestershire. Halfway there we stopped and had a picnic. After that we were off again.

At three o'clock we were on the border of Gloucestershire. At half past three we were waiting outside St. Mary's Church. Most of the family arrived with my nephew Peter, who shook my hand outside the church, and he said to me, "I am pleased you got here Joey."

My friend Ernie told Peter that I hoped my cough didn't interfere with the people in the church, and that I was worried about it. At five to four the bride walked in, that was my niece Linda. I thought she was my grandmother. I was very proud to be her uncle on her father's side. All through the wedding I was thinking to myself what a nice niece I have got. The wedding was over in less than an hour.

The bride and groom both left the church and I waved to them both. We all followed them outside the church. The photographers took photos. And they took our photo with the bride and groom. And as soon as they had finished taking photos we all went to the reception. The bride's mother spoke to us. I said to my sister-in-law that some of her family were missing. She said that she could not get anybody to look after the children.

At ten past six we got back in the car and came back to the hospital. Mr. Jenkins was a good nurse and Mr. Peckham a good driver. We arrived back at St. Lawrence's at nine o'clock. Night nurse Gino was on. I was happy to get to my bed. In May last year I said to my friend Ernie, "I'm just coming up to my fifty-third year. Half of those were silent, half were not, thanks to you. You gave me the chance to talk to the outside world." Everyone is so good to me, and the new student nurses take a great interest in me, so I hope my book will help them in their study of the spastics. In this book my friend Ernie has taken the words out of my mouth, and with the help of Tom and Michael and some of the staff put them on paper. This is the end of my autobiography. I am very grateful to all the people who helped to make it possible.